# NIKOLA TESLA
# FOR KIDS

## HIS LIFE, IDEAS, AND INVENTIONS, WITH 21 ACTIVITIES

Amy M. O'Quinn

CHICAGO
REVIEW
PRESS

Copyright © 2019 by Amy M. O'Quinn
All rights reserved
First edition
Published by Chicago Review Press Incorporated
814 North Franklin Street
Chicago, Illinois 60610
ISBN 978-0-912777-21-4

**Library of Congress Cataloging-in-Publication Data**
Names: O'Quinn, Amy M., author.
Title: Nikola Tesla for kids : his life, ideas, and inventions, with 21
   activities / Amy M. O'Quinn.
Description: First edition. | Chicago, Illinois : Chicago Review Press,
   [2019] | Audience: Ages 9+. | Includes bibliographical references and
   index.
Identifiers: LCCN 2018056856 (print) | LCCN 2018057241 (ebook) | ISBN
   9780912777221 (adobe pdf) | ISBN 9780912777238 (epub) | ISBN 9780912777245
   (kindle) | ISBN 9780912777214 (pbk.)
Subjects: LCSH: Tesla, Nikola, 1856–1943—Juvenile literature. | Serbian
   American inventors—Biography—Juvenile literature. | Electrical
   engineers—United States—Biography—Juvenile literature. |
   Inventors—United States—Biography—Juvenile literature.
Classification: LCC TK140.T4 (ebook) | LCC TK140.T4 O6925 (print) | DDC
   621.3092 [B] —dc23
LC record available at https://lccn.loc.gov/2018056856

Cover and interior design: Sarah Olson
Cover photos: (front cover, clockwise from top left) Wardenclyffe Tower: Leo
Blanchette/Shutterstock.com; Tesla's radio-controlled boat: Tesla Universe; Por-
trait of Nikola Tesla: Wikimedia Commons; Tesla with his magnifying transmit-
ter: Wikimedia Commons; Tesla's AC induction motor: Wikimedia Commons;
Tesla holding "balls of flame": University of California, Berkeley, Library; Ring
Street in Budapest: Library of Congress, LC-DIG-ppmsc-09476 DLC; (back cover)
Poster from the Paris Exposition of 1889: Wikimedia Commons; Tesla's patent
drawing 1924: United States Patent and Trademark Office; Tesla's oscillating
transformer: Wikimedia Commons
Interior illustrations: Lindsey Cleworth Schauer

Printed in the United States of America
5 4 3 2 1

*For Chad—my very own
electrical field expert*

# CONTENTS

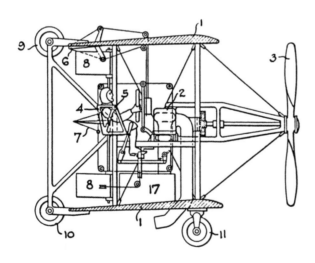

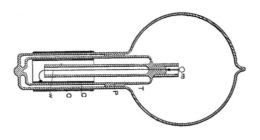

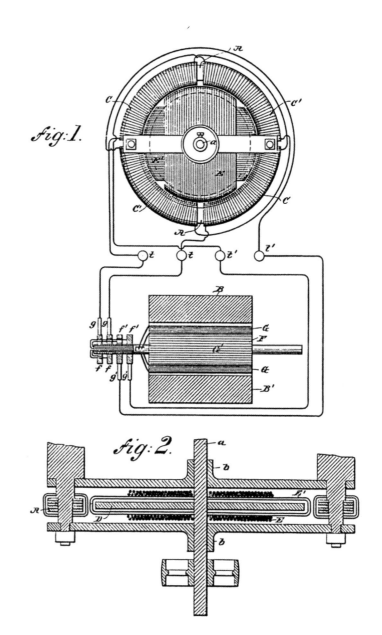

# TIME LINE

|  |  |
|------|-------|
| 1856 | July 10, Nikola Tesla is born at midnight |
| 1863 | Tesla family moves to Gospić, Croatia, where Nikola begins school |
| 1870–73 | Tesla attends the Higher Real Gymnasium in Karlovac |
| 1873 | Tesla nearly dies from cholera |
| 1875 | Tesla enrolls at the Austrian Polytechnic School in Graz |
| 1877 | Tesla sees a Gramme dynamo, begins work on AC powered motor |
| 1879 | April 17, Tesla's father, Milutin, dies |
| 1880 | Tesla studies at Charles University in Prague |
| 1881 | Tesla moves to Budapest, Hungary |
| 1882 | After a mental breakdown, Tesla has a vision of an AC motor with a rotating magnetic field |
|  | April, Tesla moves to Paris |

|  |  |
|------|-------|
| 1884 | June 6, Tesla arrives in New York |
|  | Tesla meets Thomas Edison and begins working for the Edison Electric Company |
| 1885 | Tesla quits his job with Edison Electric Light Company |
| 1885–86 | Tesla forms the Tesla Electric Light and Manufacturing Company |
| 1887–88 | Tesla forms the Tesla Electric Company |
| 1888 | Tesla demonstrates his AC motor and polyphase for the American Institute of Electrical Engineers (AIEE) |
|  | Tesla sells patents for the AC motor and polyphase to George Westinghouse |
| 1891 | Tesla invents the Tesla coil |
|  | July 30, Tesla becomes a US citizen |
| 1892 | April 4, Tesla's mother, Đuka, dies |

**1893** Westinghouse-Tesla team wins bid to light the World's Columbian Exposition

**1895** March 13, Tesla's lab burns; his equipment and research are destroyed

**1896** First AC hydroelectric power plant opens at Niagara Falls

**1899** Tesla experiments with wireless electricity transmission in Colorado Springs

**1901** Wardenclyffe construction begins on Long Island, New York

December 12, Guglielmo Marconi transmits the letter "S" across the Atlantic Ocean

**1903** July 17, J. P. Morgan withdraws financial support for Wardenclyffe project

**1904** US Patent and Trademark Office reverses decision on Tesla's radio invention, awards patent to Marconi

**1906** Tesla goes public with bladeless turbine idea

**1909** Marconi wins the Nobel Prize in Physics "in recognition of [his] contributions to the development of wireless telegraphy"

**1917** May 18, Tesla receives the Edison Medal

July 4, Wardenclyffe is demolished

**1928** Tesla receives final patent for a VTOL airplane

**1931** Tesla turns 75 and is featured on the cover of *Time* magazine

**1934** Tesla talks about his new defensive particle beam "death ray"

**1943** January 7, Tesla dies in New York at age 86

US Supreme Court rules that Tesla, not Marconi, was the true inventor of the radio; patent reinstated on June 21

# INTRODUCTION

The transatlantic crossing had been extremely uncomfortable. It was also unnerving for the young Serb, due to unrest and tension among the crew. Just as he'd prepared to board the train to leave Paris, he'd discovered that his luggage, wallet, and ticket for the voyage had been stolen. To reach the port in Liverpool before his steamship departed for America, he'd had to run alongside and jump up onto the moving train at the very last minute. Thankfully, he'd had enough change in his pocket to pay the train fare. Then he'd had to do some fast talking to get aboard the ship, convincing the ship's attendants that he really had bought a ticket. When no one else claimed his berth, they allowed him to embark.

But now, the long, unpleasant journey was finally over. When he stepped out of the Castle Garden Immigration Center in Manhattan on June 6, 1884, he had only a few coins in his pocket, several poems and articles he'd written, a packet of mathematical problems he wanted to work on, and drawings for a flying machine. But he had made it to America, the "Land of Golden Promise," and that was all that mattered.

If anyone heard him speak, they might've noted his strange, and very strong, accent. Just another immigrant, they might've presumed, one of the hundreds of thousands entering the country each year. Without another thought, they probably would've continued on their way, thinking him nothing out of the ordinary.

But they would've been mistaken. This tall, dark-haired, immaculately groomed twenty-eight-year-old gentleman weaving his way through the crowded New York streets was most assuredly someone special. And within a few years, he would be recognized and celebrated as one of the greatest thinkers and inventors of all time. His ideas and inventions would change the modern world.

His name? Nikola Tesla.

**Nikola Tesla with his magnifying transmitter in his Colorado Springs laboratory, 1899.** *Wikimedia Commons*

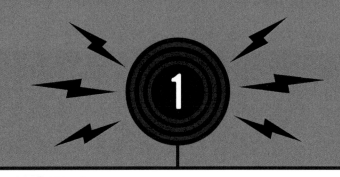

# 1

# ELECTRIFIED BEGINNINGS

*A child of light.* —Đuka Tesla

On the stroke of midnight between July 9 and 10, 1856, a newborn's cry echoed through the Tesla farmhouse near the small hamlet of Smiljan, in what is today the country of Croatia, near the Bosnian border. According to family legend, thunder rumbled and lightning flashed as a violent summer storm coincided with the baby boy's entrance into the world. The frightened, superstitious village midwife turned to the infant's mother and lamented, "He'll be a child of the storm."

"No," Đuka Tesla replied. "A child of light."

Little did the baby's mother realize how prophetic her words would be. The child born during the fierce storm that night was Nikola Tesla, and his

**The oldest known photo of Nikola Tesla's birthplace in Smiljan, taken in 1933.** *Tesla Universe*

inventions and ideas would one day electrify and revolutionize the world.

## The Teslas

The Teslas had moved to the area about a year before Nikola was born. Nikola's father, Milutin, was a Serbian Orthodox priest who'd been assigned to the church near the village of Smiljan, which was then part of the Austro-Hungarian Empire. When they first arrived at their new home in 1855, Milutin and Đuka already had one son and two daughters—Dane (pronounced DAH-nay), Angelina, and Milka. Nikola was the fourth child and second son in the family, and his youngest sister, Marica, was born in 1858. The family lived in a home next to the church, and life was full and busy with church duties, farmwork, and exploring the beautiful countryside.

Although they lived in Austrian Croatia, the Teslas were proud of their Serbian ethnicity and heritage. In fact, Nikola's paternal grandfather was an army officer who had served under Napoleon during the Serbian Revolution. Nikola's father, Milutin, had ambitions to join the military as well, but he found that philosophy, literature, and poetry were far more to his liking. Moreover, while enrolled in a military academy, he'd taken offense to being criticized by an officer for not keeping his buttons polished. At the time, the two most respected professions for educated Serbs were either military or church related, so the disillusioned Milutin decided to

**Milutin Tesla, Nikola's father.**
*Tesla Universe*

follow in the footsteps of other esteemed Tesla relatives instead and become a priest. This decision also meant that he would have the opportunity to continue his education and use his influence to call for social reform. According to Nikola, Milutin, using the pen name "Man of Justice," published editorials in local newspapers in the early years of his priesthood that called for "social equality among peoples, the need for compulsory education for children, and the creation of Serbian schools in Croatia."

Milutin's intellect and actions impressed many people, especially those who were educated themselves. The young priest also caught the attention of Đuka Mandić, a daughter from one of the most prominent land-owning Serbian families in the area. (Translated, the name Đuka means Georgina.) The two married in 1847, moved to a parish at Senj near the Adriatic Sea, and started their family.

## The Mandić Family

Like the Teslas, Đuka's family tree also included several distinguished ancestors. Her maternal grandfather, a priest named Toma Budisavljević, was presented with a French merit award called the Legion of Honour from Napoleon in 1811. Toma was recognized for his leadership when Croatia was occupied by France. One of his daughters, Soka, married a Serbian minister named Nikola Mandić, who also came from a notable military and clerical background. They had eight children, and Đuka, who was born in 1821, was the eldest.

# EXPLORE NIKOLA'S BIRTHPLACE

*The Tesla family lived in Croatia, yet they were ethnically of Serbian descent. But when Nikola was a child, Croatia was part of the massive Austro-Hungarian Empire. Serbia, which is farther east, was part of the Ottoman Empire. After World War I, Croatia and Serbia became part of a new country called Yugoslavia. But in the 1990s, Yugoslavia began separating into self-governing countries, and both Croatia and Serbia regained their names and independence.*

*Examine the map to see how the boundary lines of Europe and the Balkan Peninsula looked in the 1800s. Map and label how the same areas look today.*

--------------------------------------------------------------------------------

## You'll Need

⚡ Library or internet access
⚡ Current map of Europe showing the Balkans
⚡ Paper
⚡ Pen or marker

1. Print a current map of the Balkans as they look today. Find one online, such as the PDF at http://d-maps.com/m/europa/balkans/balkans06.pdf.

2. Use an online source to identify and label the countries of Austria, Croatia, Hungary, Serbia, and Slovenia, as well as the Adriatic, Mediterranean, and Aegean Seas. Label the following cities: Belgrade, Budapest, Gospić, Graz, Karlovac, Maribor, Sarajevo, Smiljan, and Zagreb.

3. Use this map as a reference when learning about Tesla's life and travels in southern Europe.

CIRCA 1850
OTTOMAN EMPIRE
AUSTRIAN EMPIRE

AUSTRIAN EMPIRE

CROATIA
HUNGARY
BOSNIA
Smiljan ▪
SERBIA
OTTOMAN EMPIRE
ADRIATIC SEA
MONTENEGRO
ITALY
BALKAN MOUNTAINS
ALBANIA
AEGEAN SEA
IONIAN SEA
GREECE

One of Đuka's brothers, Pajo, became a field marshal in the imperial Austro-Hungarian Army. Another Mandić ran an Austrian military academy. A third brother, Petar, entered a monastery and eventually became the regional bishop of Bosnia.

Unfortunately, the Mandićs' mother, Soka, lost her eyesight when Đuka was still quite young, and all the household duties fell upon the oldest daughter's shoulders. Because of her many responsibilities at home, Đuka was unable to go to school, and she never learned to read or write. However, she was gifted with an amazing memory, and she could recite long Bible passages and epic Serbian poems. As an adult, she became a supportive wife to her priest husband, a tireless mother to her five children, and a skilled and artistic home manager. But Đuka was also a talented inventor.

According to Nikola: "My mother descended from one of the oldest families in the country and a line of inventors. Both her father and grandfather originated numerous implements for household, agricultural, and other uses. She was a truly great woman, of rare skill, courage, and fortitude, who had braved the storms of life and past thru [sic] many a trying experience."

Almost everything in the Tesla home was a product of Đuka's hands and hard work. She was an excellent needlewoman and was well known in the area for the beautiful tapestries she embroidered. An even more unusual accomplishment was that she invented many time-saving tools to help her with her daily work, including a mechanical egg beater. According to her son, Đuka's fingers were nimble enough to tie three knots in an eyelash, even when she was past 60!

In his autobiography, Tesla credited his own inventiveness to his mother's influence. He also said, "My mother was an inventor of the first order and would, I believe, have achieved great things had she not been so remote from modern life and its multifold opportunities."

# Escapades, Exploration, and Early Inventions

All the Tesla children delighted in playing outside and roaming the countryside. In many ways, Nikola and his siblings had an idyllic childhood. There was always something to do and an adventure to be had. Nikola enjoyed animals, and in fact he often seemed to interact better with animals than people. The family cat, Mačak (the pet's name was also the Croatian word for "cat"), brought him special joy, and many years later he referred to Mačak as "the fountain of my enjoyment."

Mačak also provided young Nikola with his first experience with static electricity as he stroked the cat's back one cold, dry evening. "Mačak's back was a sheet of light and my hand produced a shower of erupting sparks loud enough to be heard all over the place. My father was a very learned man, he had an answer for every question. 'Well,' he finally remarked, 'this is nothing but electricity, the same thing you see in the trees in a storm.'" Nikola Tesla never forgot this early episode, and it triggered his imagination and lifelong fascination with electricity.

# ELECTRICITY BASICS

All matter is made up of atoms, which are the smallest particles of an element. An atom is composed of protons, neutrons, and electrons. The negatively charged electrons orbit around the nucleus, or the center of the atom, which is made up of positively charged protons and uncharged neutrons. These negative and positive charges attract to hold the atom together.

Sometimes, however, something will happen to cause an electron to break away from the atom, and this separation can create a current or flow of electricity. In fact, if the movement of electrons is controlled in a circuit, and it's powerful enough, it can do fantastic things.

For example, with millions and trillions of electrons moving along a good conductor (such as copper), they can power trains, service factories, or even light up the lamps in your home. Good conductors of electricity allow the electrons to flow easily, with little resistance. Poor conductors of electricity, such as glass, plastic, rubber, or wood, are called insulators.

There are two types of electric current—direct current (DC) and alternating current (AC).

How are they different?

The electrons in direct current flow continuously in one direction. Batteries, cell phones, and computers are all examples of items that use direct current.

The electrons in alternating current flow in both directions, alternating back and forth, many times per second. The result is that they don't actually move with the current flow. Instead, they sort of wiggle one way and then the other without really going anywhere. Most household appliances, power distribution systems, and electric and lighting circuits in homes and businesses run off alternating current.

**Direct Current (DC)**

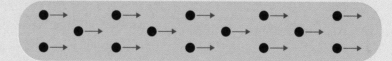

**Alternating Current (AC)**

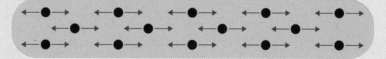

# MAKE STATIC ELECTRICITY

*Static electricity is the buildup of an electric charge on the surface of an object. The word static means stationary or still. The electric charge stays in one place rather than moving or flowing to another area. Static electricity can even build up on you! For example, have you ever rubbed your feet against carpet, then touched a doorknob? Zap! That's static electricity being transferred from one object to another.*

*See if you can spark some static electricity with this experiment.*

## You'll Need

⚡ 2 balloons (12-inch [30-centimeter] work well)

⚡ 1 string, 36 inches (91 centimeters) long

⚡ 3-inch (8-centimeter) square of 100 percent wool fabric

⚡ 1 sheet tissue paper, torn into 1-inch pieces

⚡ Plastic comb

1. Inflate and tie off two balloons.

2. Tie one balloon to each end of a 36-inch (91-centimeter) string.

3. Rub woolen fabric against one balloon and then the other.

4. Hold the string in the center, so that both balloons are hanging down, side by side. What happens?

5. Now try rubbing one of the balloons back and forth against your hair. Then slowly pull it away. What happens?

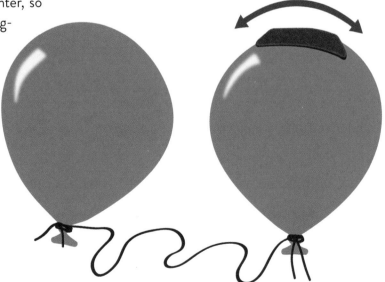

6. Now place torn tissue paper pieces on a flat surface. Run a plastic comb through your hair or rub it with woolen fabric to charge it with static electricity. Hold the comb near the tissue paper pieces.
What happens?

Rubbing the balloons against the wool or your hair gives them a negative charge. Since like charges repel each other, and both balloons have a negative charge, they will push away from each other.

When you pull the balloon away from your hair, it will make your hair rise up toward the balloon. The balloon took some of the electrons away from your hair, leaving it with a positive charge. Since opposites attract, your hair will lift up in the direction of the negatively charged balloon.

The same explanation goes for the comb and tissue paper pieces. When you pull the comb through your hair or rub it against the wool, it becomes negatively charged. The tissue paper pieces have a positive charge. Opposite charges attract, so the tissue paper pieces jump up toward the comb.

It's not magic—it's static electricity!

Nikola had his share of excitement and escapades. He had a vivid imagination and great curiosity, which got him into trouble many times as a young boy. Once he became lost and was accidentally locked up in an old country church all night, while family and friends looked for him. Another time, he fell into a vat of hot milk, which luckily had not reached a temperature high enough to scald him.

During one impassioned game, Nikola attacked his mother's cornstalks and battled them to the ground with a wooden sword, pretending to be a Serbian hero conquering his enemies. Upset that Nikola had needlessly destroyed some of the family's food sources, Đuka spanked her son and quickly ended the game. He also figured out that it was unwise to take apart his grandfather's clocks when he did not know the secret to putting them back together again. More punishment followed when he broke several farmhouse windows while firing his homemade cornstalk popgun.

Due to his interest in the barnyard chickens and other birds, Nikola became fascinated by the idea of flight and decided to try it out for himself. He took an umbrella and climbed to the top of the barn. Believing that the umbrella would work like a parachute and allow him to gently drift down to the ground, he jumped. The disastrous experiment resulted in a fall that shook him up badly. Although no bones were broken, Nikola spent the next six weeks in bed recovering from his bruises and the bad experience.

Nikola also liked to tell a humorous family story about two of his elderly aunts. They both had wrinkled faces, but one had "two teeth protruding like the tusks of an elephant which she buried in my cheek every time she kissed me." Nikola did not care for his aunts' displays of affection at all, preferring instead to stay in his mother's arms.

## NIKOLA'S FIRST INVENTION

A village boy had received a hook and fishing tackle, and all the boys, except Nikola, who'd quarreled with the hook's owner, started out to catch frogs. Tesla described the excursion later in life:

*I never had seen a hook . . . but, prompted by necessity, I got hold of a piece of soft iron wire, bent it, and sharpened it by means of two stones. Then I attached it to a strong string, cut a rod, gathered bait, and went to the brook, where the frogs were innumerable.*

*In vain I tried to capture the frogs in the water; and I was humiliated to think what a big catch my playmates would bring home with their fine tackle. But at last I dangled my empty hook in front of a frog sitting on a stump, and I can see now in my mind's eye what happened as vividly as though it were yesterday.*

*First, the frog collapsed, then his eyes bulged, and he swelled to twice his normal size, made a vicious snap at the hook—and I pulled him in. . . . I went home with a fine catch, whereas my playmates caught none. To this day I consider my frog-hook invention quite remarkable and very ambitious.*

Once when asked which was the prettier of the two aunts, he thought for a moment, then pointed at one of them, saying, "This here is not as ugly as the other."

At age four, Nikola constructed a smooth wooden disk and made an axle out of a twig. When he lowered the disk into a stream, he was delighted when it began to turn with the current. This would be the same principle behind his future invention of the bladeless turbine.

He also came up with the idea to build a propeller powered by four live June bugs (or May bugs as Nikola called them). He glued one June bug to each of the four thin wooden blades, which were arranged on a spindle in the form of a cross. When the insects tried to fly away, the power created by the whirling of their wings caused the propeller to turn rapidly.

Nikola was thrilled with his discovery—at first. Then the son of a visiting retired Austrian military officer pulled the bugs off the propeller blades one by one, popped them into his mouth, and began to chew. Nikola was appalled. Later he said, "That disgusting sight terminated my endeavors in this promising field and I have never since been able to touch a May-bug [June bug] or any other insect for that matter."

Nikola began attending the small village school when he was five, and he loved to read. Milutin had a large home library, but he did not allow young Nikola to touch his books. But such was the boy's passion for reading that he snuck into the forbidden room every chance he got. Then, when his parents worried that reading by candlelight at night might damage his eyesight, he secretly took candles to his room without their knowledge. When Milutin found out, he hid all the candles. Undaunted, Nikola found a way around the problem. He covertly gathered up all the necessary supplies and made his own candles! Each night while everyone else slept, he plugged the keyhole and cracks around his bedroom door to block the light, lit a candle, and often read until dawn.

## Tragedy and Change

Nikola's older brother, Dane, was his parents' pride and joy—the family genius. He was exceptionally gifted, and his personality, talent, and intelligence apparently far overshadowed that of his brother, who was five years younger. But tragedy struck when Dane was 12. He was thrown from the family's Arabian horse and died from his injuries a few days later.

Apparently, Nikola saw the accident, and some historians have speculated that he may have inadvertently spooked the horse, causing the animal to rear and throw his brother. Regardless of how it happened, Dane's death profoundly affected the whole Tesla family, but especially Nikola. He always felt a responsibility to fill the void left by Dane's death, but he never believed that he measured up to his brother's brilliance. Nikola later wrote, "The recollection of [Dane's] attainments made every effort of mine seem dull in comparison. Anything I did that was creditable merely caused my parents to feel their loss more keenly. So I grew up with little confidence in myself."

A panoramic view of Gospić and the Lika River. *Wikimedia Commons*

Not long after Dane's death, Milutin was promoted to a larger church in Gospić, a city several miles from Smiljan. Nikola began attending the elementary school there, but the adjustment was extremely hard for him. He'd been used to freely roaming the mountainous countryside and exploring the natural world, but in Gospić he felt closed in by his urban surroundings and confused by the way things were done in the city. He considered the change of residence to be a "calamity." He said, "In our new house, I was but a prisoner, watching the strange people I saw thru the window blinds. I would rather have faced a roaring lion than one of the city dudes who strolled about."

Not long after the family's relocation to Gospić, visions—appearances of strange images and objects—began to plague Nikola's mind. Some psychologists today believe that the emotional stress of witnessing Dane's death may have triggered some of these mental phenomena, or perhaps it was just the way Nikola's brain worked. In any case, the visions caused him great anxiety. He already knew he was different from other children, and he didn't want to further embarrass his family by talking about these odd experiences.

Many years later, he described what he'd dealt with in his younger days: "In my boyhood I suffered from a peculiar affliction to the appearance of images, often accompanied by strong flashes of light, which marred the sight of real images and interfered with my thought and action. They were pictures of things and scenes which I had really seen, never of those I imagined. When a word was spoken to me the image of the object it designated would present itself vividly to my vision and sometimes I was quite unable to distinguish whether what I saw was tangible or not."

Tesla never believed that his visions were hallucinations but rather that they were "the result of a reflex action from the brain on the retina under great excitation."

He also recalled that as he lay in bed at night and closed his eyes, he would sometimes witness a "funeral or some such nerve-wracking spectacle." As the problem continued, he tried to make these visions stop by using his imagination; he made excursions in his mind to places he'd never been before. Over time he began to see new scenes that were blurry at first and would "flit away" when he tried to concentrate on them. Eventually, these places became more concrete and real to Nikola, and he gained great comfort from the new, less troubling visions as he traveled in his mind. "Every night (and sometimes during the day), when alone, I would start on my journey and make friendships and acquaintances and, however unbelievable, it is a fact that they were just as dear to me as those in actual life and not a bit less intense in their manifestations."

These mind-traveling occurrences continued until Nikola was about 17 years old, when he seriously turned his attention to inventing. Then, to his delight, he found that he could use the very same power to envision and create models and inventions in his mind, and these images were as real to him as physical things he could hold in his hands. This ability would later prove to be a gift—and a hindrance—to his career.

In addition to these strange mental phenomena, Nikola also developed puzzling habits and strong aversions to certain things that lasted his whole life. Many modern psychologists agree that he probably had obsessive-compulsive disorder (OCD). He experienced a "violent aversion" to women's earrings and pearls (although he found other jewelry pleasing), certain smells, and objects with smooth surfaces. Moreover, he stated that just looking at a peach could give him a fever, and he could never stand to touch anyone's hair. He also wouldn't shake others' hands, and he threw away gloves after wearing them for only a week.

Years later he wrote of other obsessions that he experienced in adulthood: "I counted the steps in my walks and calculated the cubical contents of soup plates, coffee cups, and pieces of food—otherwise my meal was unenjoyable. All repeated acts or operations I performed had to be divisible by three and if I missed I felt impelled to do it all over again, even if it took hours."

While young Nikola was struggling with his troubling visions, Milutin was concerned about making a favorable impression on his new congregation at the church with the "onion-shaped dome" in Gospić. He wanted his children to be good examples, especially Nikola, on whom he now pinned the hopes of becoming a priest, since Dane had died. Milutin always made sure they were dressed in their finest clothing to attend Sunday services and demonstrated their very best manners and behavior.

Nikola, still upset about the family's move to Gospić, had no desire to mingle with the strange parishioners, so he was relieved when his father gave him the job of climbing the belfry to ring the bell. From this high-up position, he could see the people making their way to the church, but he stayed in the tower until he thought the service was over and all the people were gone.

Unfortunately, on one Sunday, as he came running down the belfry stairs two or three at a time, a wealthy lady wearing a beautiful floor-length gown was exiting the church and making her way to shake Milutin's hand. Nikola accidentally stepped upon her skirt's long train brushing along the ground behind her and tore it from the

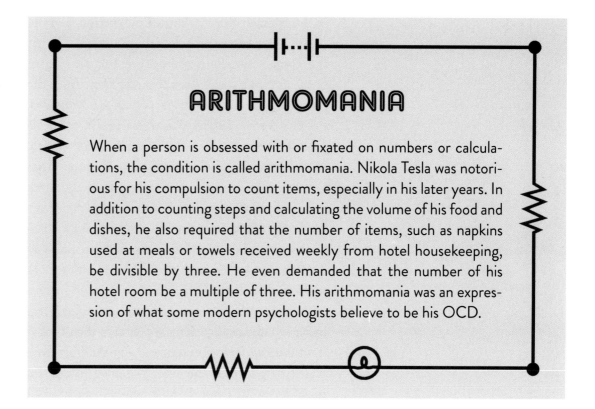

## ARITHMOMANIA

When a person is obsessed with or fixated on numbers or calculations, the condition is called arithmomania. Nikola Tesla was notorious for his compulsion to count items, especially in his later years. In addition to counting steps and calculating the volume of his food and dishes, he also required that the number of items, such as napkins used at meals or towels received weekly from hotel housekeeping, be divisible by three. He even demanded that the number of his hotel room be a multiple of three. His arithmomania was an expression of what some modern psychologists believe to be his OCD.

dress. He was horrified, and his father was furious! According to Tesla's first biographer, John J. O'Neill, "He was practically ostracized by the parishioners, and continued so until he redeemed himself in a spectacular manner."

Apparently, a year later, a new fire department was established in Gospić to replace the outdated bucket brigade system that was still used to fight fires. The firefighters had snappy, colorful uniforms and a brand-new pump operated by 16 men. All the townspeople turned out for a riverfront demonstration of the beautiful red-and-black pump. It was a celebratory event with speeches and a dedication. Like everyone else, Nikola watched as the men got ready to show how the pump could shoot water from the nozzle high into the air. At the signal, everyone waited breathlessly. Then, nothing. Not a single drop of water came from the pump's nozzle.

The embarrassed fire department officials adjusted the handles, disconnected the hoses, reconnected the hoses, and tried to find the problem. Professors and experts stepped in and tried other solutions. But still nothing happened. Suddenly, Nikola had an idea. He told the men to keep pumping, and then he ran to the river, stripped off his Sunday clothes, and jumped in. He found the suction hose that was supposed to draw the water into the line and discovered it was kinked and had collapsed due to the vacuum action of the pump.

Nikola quickly straightened out the hose, and water rushed into the line. A powerful stream gushed from the nozzle, shot upward, and rained down on the heads of unsuspecting officials and townspeople. But everyone was happy, and Nikola became the hero of the day—his previous mistake was all but forgotten! He also received a valuable lesson that day: "Tesla learned that solving technical problems could lead to recognition and approval."

## Complete Control

After Dane's death and the family's move to Gospić, another interesting thing happened that profoundly affected Nikola's thoughts and actions. He'd always been introspective and worried that he might have a weak character. He also fretted over his lack of self-control. But when he was around age 12, he found a book in his father's library that would change his life. It was a Serbian translation of a historical novel, *Abafi*, penned in 1836 by a Hungarian writer named Miklós Jósika. The young male character in the book used willpower and self-control to overcome his problems and become a national hero. Greatly inspired, Nikola decided to use the same ideas and principles in his own life.

He later wrote, "I began to discipline myself. Had I a sweet cake or a juicy apple which I was dying to eat I would give it to another boy . . . pained but satisfied. Had I some difficult task before me which was exhausting I would attack it again and again until it was done."

It was hard at first, but soon he was able to conquer what he saw as his weaknesses. He said he found pleasure in "doing as [he] willed." From then on, self-denial and willpower were always part of Tesla's life, and he believed these traits were the key to his success as an inventor.

## Growing Up

At age 10, Nikola entered the Real Gymnasium, the equivalent of middle school or junior high, in Gospić. He was very skilled in both math and science, and he excelled in his studies—especially in physics. Nikola first saw mechanical models in his physics class, and he was fascinated by them. He also saw an engraving of Niagara Falls and read a description of the giant waterfalls. According to biographer Margaret Cheney, "In his imagination, a big wheel appeared, run by the cascading waters. He told his uncle that one day he would go to America and carry out this vision."

Nikola enjoyed working in the well-equipped physics department at the Real Gymnasium. "I was interested in electricity almost from the beginning of my educational career," he wrote. "I read all that I could find on the subject . . . [and] experimented with batteries and induction coils."

Nikola also used his talent for imagining everything down to the smallest detail in his mind's eye. He could do math problems quickly, visualizing each step, without writing down his calculations. This ability amazed his math teachers. Unfortunately, though, he had extremely poor grades in the required drawing class, and he found the assignments very hard. The rest of his family members were very skilled in drawing; perhaps his difficulty was because he was left-handed and all the desks and equipment were geared to right-handers. Whatever the reason, Nikola struggled, and even in later years he never liked to draw sketches of his inventions or ideas, which caused problems when trying to convey his thoughts to others.

Unsurprisingly, teachers noticed young Nikola's strengths in the areas of technology and physics and encouraged his interest. He happily researched and explored countless scientific ideas and inventions—even the crazy concept of a flying machine! He began to consider pursuing a scientific career, but Milutin insisted that his only living son would become a priest. Nikola was disappointed but resigned.

Perhaps it was because he put intense pressure on himself to succeed, but Nikola became extremely ill in 1870, right after he finished his schooling at the Real Gymnasium. He said, "[I] was prostrated with a dangerous illness or rather, a score of them, and my condition became so desperate that I was given up by physicians."

Because his parents didn't know if he would live, Nikola was finally allowed to read as many books as he wished, both those from his father's vast collection and the local library. He quite enjoyed "a few volumes of new literature unlike anything I had ever read before and so captivating as to make me utterly forget my hopeless state." Nikola claimed that the books prompted "the miraculous recovery that followed," especially early works by American author Samuel Langhorne Clemens—better known by his pen name, Mark Twain. Twenty-five years later, the two men would become great friends, and when he was told of the event, Twain was said to have "burst into tears."

Whatever the cause or the cure, 14-year-old Nikola's health was restored, and in 1870 he moved to Karlovac to attend a new four-year high school program, called the Higher Real Gymnasium. He would be able take more advanced courses than those offered at the Gospić school. At the new school, his physics professor, Martin Sekulić, first introduced him to the principle of electromagnetic induction, which makes the generation of electricity possible.

Nikola lived with his father's sister, Stanka, and her husband, Colonel Branković. Nikola called this uncle "an old war horse." Apparently, Aunt

# BUILD A SIMPLE ELECTRIC CIRCUIT

*The path an electric current takes as it flows is called a circuit. You can make a direct current (DC) circuit using batteries, a bulb, and wire. Electrons in this type of circuit always flow one way, make a complete loop, then return to their starting point—like a car going around a racetrack. Unless the circuit is broken, the electrons will continue flowing around this loop.*

**ADULT SUPERVISION REQUIRED**

## You'll Need

⚡ Pliers

⚡ 3 pieces of insulated copper wire, 7 inches (18 centimeters) long

⚡ Electrical tape

⚡ 2 D-size batteries

⚡ 1 piece of corrugated cardboard, approximately 10 by 14 inches (25 by 36 centimeters)

⚡ 3 metal thumbtacks

⚡ 1 metal paper clip

⚡ 1 wooden clothespin with metal spring

⚡ 1 flashlight bulb

⚡ Wooden toothpick (optional)

1. Use a pair of pliers to gently strip about 1 inch (3 centimeters) of the plastic coating or insulation from both ends of all three pieces of wire. Ask an adult to help.

2. Use electrical tape to tape two D batteries together, end to end, with the negative end of one battery touching the positive end of the other battery.

3. Tape this battery "pack" to one side of the of corrugated cardboard.

4. Tape the end of a piece of wire to one end of the battery pack. Carefully wrap the other end of that wire around the post of a thumbtack.

5. Hook one end of a metal paperclip around the thumbtack and press the thumbtack down into the cardboard surface. You want the paperclip to be able to rotate back and forth.

6. Wrap each end of a second piece of wire around two more thumbtacks. Stretch out the wire so it's opposite but parallel to the battery pack.

7. Press one thumbtack down into the cardboard. Place it close enough to be touched by the paperclip as it swings around. This opening and closing motion

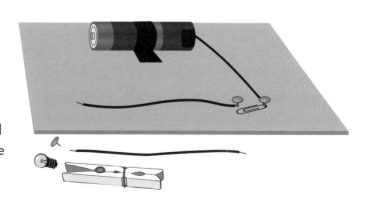

forms a rotating switch. After testing the placement, leave the switch in the open position (not touching the tack).

8. Tape one end of the last piece of wire to the other end of the battery pack. Wrap the other end of the wire around the last thumbtack (which will now be connected to two wires) and press it into the cardboard.

9. Position the clothespin over this last thumbtack, then pinch the tack in the clothespin so the pin is flush with the cardboard.

10. Secure the flashlight bulb in the clothespin over the thumbtack, so the bottom of the bulb is touching the thumbtack.

11. Close the switch by touching the paperclip to the thumbtacks on each end. What happens?

12. Now open the switch so only one end of the paperclip is touching a thumbtack. Does anything change?

When the paperclip switch is touching a metal thumbtack on each end, the circuit is complete, or closed. The bulb lights up. When the paperclip is touching metal on only one end, the circuit is not complete and the bulb will not light up. An electrical circuit must be closed and complete before the electrons and electricity will flow around the loop and light the bulb.

Try substituting other items in place of the paperclip. Look for good conductors—such as a hair pin or a key—which will complete the circuit. Also try insulators—a wooden toothpick, for example—which will interrupt the flow of electricity.

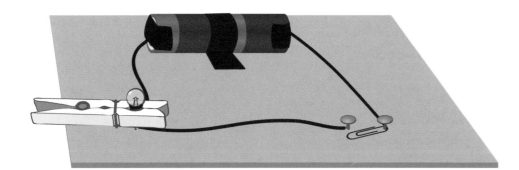

Stanka ran a very rigid and disciplined home, but she was reluctant to serve large meals, as she proclaimed Nikola's health to be "very delicate." He was constantly hungry, yet he noted that he learned to appreciate an "atmosphere of refinement and artistic taste quite unusual for those times and conditions."

Nikola was an eager student, and he completed the four-year course of study in only three years. And since Milutin still insisted that it was his son's duty to become a priest, Nikola reluctantly made plans to return home to fulfill his parents' wishes. However, right before he was to leave, he received a confusing message from his father telling him to go on a hunting expedition in the mountains instead of coming home. Nikola soon learned that a terrible cholera epidemic had broken out in Gospić; the "streets were stacked with corpses, the atmosphere thick with smoke, for the people mistakenly thought that cholera was being transmitted through the air rather than by drinking water."

Disobeying his father's instructions, Nikola went home to Gospić anyway and quickly came down with the dreaded, deadly cholera. He was bedridden for nine months, but amazingly the disease proved to be a major turning point in Nikola's future. During one particularly terrible phase of the illness, when recovery seemed impossible, he told Milutin, "Perhaps I may get well if you let me study engineering."

Probably terrified of losing another son, Milutin put aside his own hopes and plans to give his sick child something to live for. He assured Nikola that if he recovered, he would be allowed to attend and study at the best technical institute in the world. With the mysterious cure of a "bitter decoction of a peculiar bean" and the heavy weight of becoming a priest lifted from his mind, Nikola soon got well. He later stated, "I came to life like another Lazarus to the utter amazement of everybody."

True to his word, Milutin arranged for Nikola to attend the Austrian Polytechnic School in Graz. (Today, the school is known as the Graz University of Technology.) But before heading off to college, he spent a year roaming and living in the mountains and studying nature. This sabbatical was supposed to make him "stronger in body as well as mind," but modern historians think there was more to it. War had broken out with Turkey, and the Austrian government wanted all able young men to serve in the military for three years. So, perhaps Milutin, who was a pacifist, told his son to pack his gear, head for the hills, and lay low to avoid being drafted—and, of course, to have time to fully regain his health as well.

Nikola thought up many new inventions during his months in the wild, including a "submarine tube . . . [able] to convey letters and packages across the seas . . . [and] a ring around the equator" for transporting people from one end of the globe to another.

When the year was up, Nikola returned home in 1875. According to biographer Bernard Carlson, Nikola was awarded a partial scholarship from the "Military Frontier Administration Authority (Grenzlandsverwaltungsbehoerde)." Therefore, he traveled to Graz, ready to begin his college education.

## A Higher Education

The Austrian Polytechnic School in Graz was considered one of the very best institutes in the Austrian empire for students studying science and engineering, and 19-year-old Nikola nearly drove himself to the point of exhaustion with his course load and hours of study. He was determined to succeed and excel, but he also wanted to "give his parents a surprise" with all he could accomplish during his first year. In his autobiography, he wrote, "I regularly started my work at three o'clock in the morning and continued until eleven at night, no Sundays or holidays excepted. As most of my fellow-students took things easily, naturally enough I eclipsed all records."

When he triumphantly returned home for a short break at the end of his first year, Nikola expected his father to be impressed with his exceptional grades and the nine flattering exam certificates from his professors. Instead, he was mortified when Milutin "made light of these hard-won honors." Instead of praise, Nikola received criticism from his father for working too hard. Nikola was upset by Milutin's displeasure, and the incident almost destroyed his ambition and caused a rift between father and son.

Many years later, after his father died, Nikola found letters that his professors had written to his parents, expressing their concern that he (Nikola)

might kill himself from overwork and too little sleep if something wasn't done. They recommended he leave the Polytechnic School, and Milutin must have agreed, as he discouraged Nikola from returning the second year. Although Nikola didn't know about the professors' correspondence or the reasons for his father's disapproval, he disregarded Milutin's wishes and made plans to go back to Graz anyway.

Nikola had originally planned to become a math professor, so during the first year he'd taken courses in arithmetic, geometry, physics, calculus, chemistry, mineralogy, machinery construction, botany, wave theory, optics, French, and English. He even started a club for Serbian students that lasted decades after he left Graz.

It wasn't long, however, before Nikola changed his major to engineering and added other courses to his schedule, including more languages. He also studied the works of writers such as Descartes, Goethe, and Shakespeare, learning long passages by heart.

Since he was now a full-time engineering student, Nikola decided to limit his studies to physics, mechanics, and mathematics during his second year. This gave him much more time to focus on specific scientific concepts and ideas—and get more rest.

## The Path to Discovery Begins

In January 1877, one of the physics instructors, Professor Jacob Poeschl, introduced the class to

**A Gramme dynamo.** *Wikimedia Commons*

a new machine that had just been delivered from Paris, and it would ultimately set Nikola on the course to his greatest discovery.

The Gramme machine, which was designed and patented in 1870 by a Belgian engineer named Zénobe Gramme, could operate as either a dynamo or motor. The device had a crank or handle, which when turned could work as a dynamo to generate electricity. Yet, when the machine was supplied with electricity from another source, it could work as a motor to produce mechanical power.

The Gramme machine was equipped with a commutator (a switch that reverses the flow of electric current) to ensure it would produce direct current (DC) electricity, but the wire brushes that had to be used for the process caused a great deal of sparking. Nikola watched Professor Poeschl demonstrate the electrical transmission of power using the Gramme machine as a motor, then voiced his opinion. Since he already knew that electricity in its natural state is alternating, wouldn't it be easier just to do away with the commutator altogether and simply use alternating current (AC)?

The professor quickly denounced Nikola's suggestion as preposterous and impossible. He even spent the rest of the class lecturing on the subject and thoroughly embarrassed his young student by saying, "Mr. Tesla may accomplish great things, but he certainly will never do this."

This was a challenge! Nikola didn't have an immediate answer to the problem, but he was convinced he was right and "undertook the task with all the fire and boundless confidence of youth." He would spend the next four years visualizing possibilities and trying to unravel the answer to prove Professor Poeschl wrong.

## Struggles

As an all-or-nothing thinker, Nikola became fixated on finding a solution to the alternating current problem. This mental obsession taxed his brain constantly. Moreover, he was bored with his studies, and many of the other students were jealous of his academic abilities and friendships with some of the professors. Unfortunately, Nikola began gambling at cards, billiards, and chess to deal with the stress and get away from his problems.

He returned to the Austrian Polytechnic School for a third year in the fall of 1877, but he soon stopped attending lectures. There is no record of Nikola's attendance in the spring of 1878, and it's unclear exactly what happened at this point. Some sources say he lost his scholarship because of his gambling. Others say that the Military Frontier Administration Authority, which had provided his scholarship, was abolished, and the money was no longer available.

Whatever the reason, Nikola was unable to secure a loan or get another scholarship, and he was too ashamed to tell his parents. Without a word to anyone, he left Graz in late 1878 and moved to the city of Maribor, which was about 45 miles away. He found work as a draftsman, but the job didn't last long. He eventually ended up living in a nearby coastal village. His family and friends were frantic with worry, as they had no idea where he was.

Sometime in early 1879, Nikola's old roommate passed through Maribor and saw his friend in a pub, playing cards for money. Nikola was not happy to see his pal and made it clear that he had no intention of returning to school. The roommate moved on, but he did send word back to Gospić to inform Nikola's parents of their son's whereabouts. It wasn't long before the elder Tesla showed up.

Milutin pleaded. He argued. He commanded that Nikola return to Graz. The young man refused. Milutin then suggested that Nikola consider going to the Charles University in Prague to finish his education there. The idea was immediately rejected.

Of course, Milutin was also disappointed and angry about his son's gambling habit, but Nikola simply told his father that he could stop anytime he wanted to. Unable to reason with his son on any level, Milutin returned home alone and soon became seriously ill.

A few weeks after his father's visit, Nikola was arrested by the police in Maribor as a "vagrant" and deported back to Gospić. Heartbroken to see his son brought back by the police, Milutin passed away on April 17, 1879, at age 60.

With nowhere else to go, Nikola stayed with his mother in Gospić after his father's funeral. But he continued to gamble, sometimes going for 24 hours straight. Đuka decided to handle her son differently than his father had.

Tesla wrote in his autobiography, "One afternoon, I remember, when I had lost all my money and was craving for a game, she came to me with a roll of bills and said, 'Go enjoy yourself. The sooner you lose all we possess the better it will be. I know that you will get over it.'"

Ashamed and determined, Nikola won back all the money he'd lost, and then conquered his addiction. He claimed that he was never again tempted by any form of gambling, although he was known to play a great game of billiards when he immigrated to the United States.

In the summer of 1880, 23-year-old Nikola honored his father's wish and enrolled at the Charles University in Prague, in what is now the Czech Republic. Along with his math and science studies, he continued to puzzle over the idea of building an AC motor—but the solution still eluded him. His uncles initially tried to help support him financially, but gradually they stopped sending money. Perhaps they thought it was time for him to take care of himself.

With no way to pay for tuition, he dropped out of school after only one term, never to return or earn a degree. He was determined to make it on his own, so he knew he had to find a job. And since he'd heard from an uncle that a new telephone system was being installed in Hungary by a family friend named Ferenc Puskás, Nikola packed his belongings in January 1881 and headed for Budapest.

# MOVING TO AMERICA

*I would not give my rotating field discovery for a thousand inventions, however valuable. . . . A thousand years hence, the telephone and the motion picture camera may be obsolete, but the principle of the rotating magnetic field will remain a vital, living thing.* —Nikola Tesla

**N**ikola Tesla arrived in Budapest ready to work, but unfortunately, the new telephone system he'd heard about wasn't up and running yet. So, desperate for money, he found a job at the Central Telegraph Office of Hungary, working as a draftsman for five dollars a week. The position was not ideal, and Tesla was often bored, but it did give him practical experience with electrical work.

**Ring Street in Budapest in the late 1800s.** *Views of the Austro-Hungarian Empire collection, Prints and Photographs Division, Library of Congress, LC-DIG-ppmsc-09476 DLC*

During his time at the Central Telegraph Office, Tesla made improvements on several apparatuses, but he was more obsessed with finding the answer to running a Gramme machine without a commutator. He wanted to do away with the need to have a switch to reverse the electrical current. He continued to believe that using alternating current (AC) as the power source was the answer, but the stress of finding the solution was frustrating, and eventually he suffered a "complete breakdown of nerves."

Tesla's senses had always been extremely sharp, but this breakdown apparently made them even more so. Years later, he claimed that he "could hear the ticking of a watch from three rooms away. A fly lighting on a table in his room caused a dull thud in his ear. A carriage passing a few miles away seemed to shake his whole body. A train whistle twenty miles distant made the chair on which he sat vibrate so strongly that the pain became unbearable. The ground under his feet was constantly trembling. In order for him to rest, rubber cushions were placed under his bed."

One biographer stated that in Tesla's case, "the air itself hurt." Yet, in addition to this strange physical affliction, Tesla was also severely depressed and convinced that he was dying. Thankfully, his friend and coworker Anthony Szigeti tried to help. He insisted that Tesla get up out of his bed and go outdoors for exercise and fresh air. He was also a good sounding board for Tesla's ideas for an improved motor.

# A Revelation

When the two friends were walking in City Park and reciting poetry right about sunset one evening, Tesla had a breakthrough. He'd always been able to memorize long passages of text and even entire books with ease. But on this day, he was reciting Johann Wolfgang von Goethe's *Faust* and noted that the setting sun reminded him of these lines:

> *The glow retreats, done is the day of toil;*
> *It yonder hastes, new fields of life exploring;*
> *Ah, that no wing can lift me from the soil,*
> *Upon its track to follow, follow soaring!*
> *[. . .]*
> *A glorious dream! though now the glories fade.*
> *Alas! the wings that lift the mind no aid*
> *Of wings to lift the body can bequeath me.*

Years later, he dramatically claimed, "As I uttered these inspiring words the idea came like a flash of lightning and in an instant, the truth was revealed." Using a stick, he drew a picture of his AC motor in the sand to show Szigeti his new creation and how a rotating magnetic field could make it work.

"The images were wonderfully sharp and clear and had the solidity of metal and stone, so much so that I told him, 'See my motor here; watch me reverse it.' I cannot begin to describe my emotions." He also stated, "It was a mental state of happiness about as complete as I have ever known.

. . . In less than two months I evolved virtually all the types of motor modifications of the system which are now identified with my name."

It would take Tesla several years to create a prototype for his complete AC motor system (which included dynamos, transformers, and other necessary devices) and secure the patents. But he'd finally figured out the puzzle that had perplexed him for so long, and his health and inventive zeal were restored. He now had a design and mental vision for creating alternating current technology that he knew had the potential to change the field of electrical engineering forever.

## On to Paris

Once the Budapest telephone exchange was finally in operation, the owner and family friend, Ferenc Puskás, hired Tesla to help him install the new system. Always up for a new challenge, he "threw himself into improving the exchange and even developed a new telephone repeater and amplifier." But by 1882, Ferenc had decided to sell his telephone exchange to a Budapest businessman at a profit. Tesla once again needed a job.

It didn't take long! While Ferenc was busy in Budapest, his brother and business partner, Tivadar, had been in Paris helping to introduce the city to Thomas Edison's incandescent lighting system. At Tivadar Puskás's invitation, both Nikola Tesla and Anthony Szigeti moved to Paris to work for the Continental Edison Company. Like most people, Tesla had heard about Thomas Edison and his many accomplishments, and he jumped at the chance to work for a company associated with the famous American inventor.

Edison had, in fact, sent his right-hand man, Charles Batchelor, to Paris in 1881 to organize the company for manufacturing and installing Edison lighting systems. French law dictated that any inventions patented in France also had to be manufactured there. So it was that Tesla's first connection to Edison was through his closest business associate, and, in turn, Batchelor was quickly impressed by the young Serbian engineer's intellect and skill. Therefore, not long after he arrived in Paris, Tesla was put to work designing dynamos for installing incandescent lighting.

Tesla was now making a decent living at 300 francs a month, but he would never be a good money manager and usually spent his income as soon as it was received. In fact, one biographer quoted Tesla as saying that when Tivadar Puskás asked how he was making it in Paris, he described the situation accurately with the statement that "the last twenty-nine days of the month are the toughest."

Regardless, he discovered that his new job also helped him in other ways. His AC system was still just a grand idea in his head when he left Budapest, but while working for the Continental Edison

**Nikola Tesla, age 23, circa 1879.**
*Tesla Universe*

# NIKOLA TESLA'S ORIGINAL VISION— PRINCIPLES OF THE AC INDUCTION MOTOR

Magnets have two poles: north and south. Opposite poles are attracted to each other, while like poles repel, or push away, from each other. In other words, the north pole on one magnet will always attract the south pole on another magnet. But the north pole of a magnet will always repel the north pole of another magnet.

In an AC motor, a stationary (unmoving) part called a stator contains a set of electromagnets. The stator, the section that does not move, forms the outside part of the motor. When electricity is supplied, the poles of stator magnets constantly switch from north to south, and back again—over and over.

On the inside of the motor is a moving part called the rotor, and it too contains a set of magnets. The constant switching of the polarity on the stator's electromagnets attracts the magnets on the rotor, causing it to turn very rapidly. The spinning rotor creates power that can run machines that are connected to the AC motor. The rotating magnetic field is what causes the AC motor to operate.

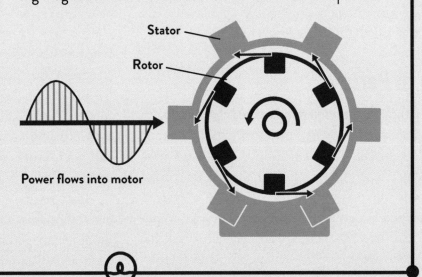

Stator

Rotor

Power flows into motor

Company, he gained practical, hands-on knowledge about dynamos and motors. This knowledge put him in a position to start thinking about converting his motor idea into a real machine.

Tesla liked to share his ideas and plans with his bosses and coworkers for creating his future AC system, which he'd decided would combine two or more separate (polyphase) AC currents that were out of step or phase with each other by 90 degrees. This meant there would also always be at least one current strong enough during each phase to keep the magnetic field moving.

To Tesla's disappointment, few of the men wanted to hear about this far-fetched, non-DC

# CREATE AN ELECTROMAGNET

*A regular magnet is permanently magnetic—you can't just turn the charge on or off. But an electromagnet is magnetic only when it is supplied with electricity, and you can easily change the strength of the electromagnet by changing the amount of electricity that flows through it. Find out for yourself!*

## You'll Need

⚡ 1 steel nail, at least 3 inches (8 centimeters) long

⚡ 32 inches (81 centimeters) thin, coated copper wire, with 1 inch (3 centimeters) of plastic coating stripped from each end

⚡ 2 D-size batteries

⚡ Electrical tape

⚡ 10 metal paper clips

1. Wind 32 inches (81 centimeters) of wire tightly around a steel nail, starting 6 inches (15 centimeters) from the end of the wire. Don't overlap the coils. Leave at least 6 inches (15 centimeters) of tail at the end, and make sure the pointed end of the nail is exposed.

2. Use electrical tape to attach one of the bare wire ends to the negative terminal of one of the batteries. Tape the other bare wire end to the positive terminal of the same battery. This is your electromagnet.

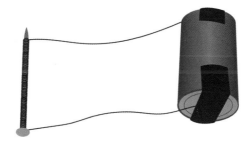

3. Put paper clips on a flat surface. Hold the battery part of the electromagnet in one hand and the wire-coiled nail carefully in the other. Lower the pointed end of the nail down over the metal paper clips. What happens?

4. Untape one end of the wire from the battery and try again. What happens this time?

5. Do the experiment again by taping two batteries end to end, negative to positive. Do more batteries make the electromagnet stronger?

6. **Safety Note: Un-tape the wire from the batteries when you are finished.**

Electricity and magnetism are closely related. With the copper wire attached to both ends of the battery, you have a circuit. The electrons flow through the wire conductor, from one end to the other, and create a current—which creates a magnetic field. All the tiny steel atoms in the nail are rearranged to point in the same direction, thus magnetizing and enabling it to attract the metal paper clips. When you disconnect the battery, however, the magnetic field disappears, and the paper clips fall off the nail.

# SEE A MAGNETIC FIELD PATTERN

*Magnetized objects that are moved into an area near a magnet will be affected by that magnet's ability to attract or repel. This area around the magnet is called its magnetic field, and a more powerful magnet will have a larger magnetic field. A magnetic field is invisible, but with this experiment, you can see what it looks like.*

## You'll Need

⚡ Strong bar magnet

⚡ Sheet of thin white card stock

⚡ Iron filings (A 12-ounce plastic shaker bottle of iron filings can be purchased online or in some hobby or discount stores.)

⚡ Pencil and scrap paper

1. Place a strong bar magnet on a flat surface.

2. Sprinkle iron filings evenly onto a sheet of card stock, then hold the card stock firmly with both hands about 2½ inches (6 centimeters) above the magnet.

3. Slowly move the cardstock down closer to the magnet. What happens to the iron filings? Do you see a pattern forming?

4. Draw what you see. Be sure to label the north and south poles of the magnet on your drawing.

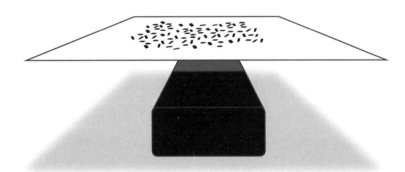

As you move the card stock holding the iron filings closer to the bar magnet, the filings will shift to create a pattern that outlines the magnetic field around the magnet. The arrangement of the filings is symmetrical (a mirror image) on both the north and south poles of the magnet. The curvy bands you see are called the lines of force, or flux. However, you'll notice that the magnetic field is strongest where the flux lines are the closest together. Sometimes you must gently tap the bottom of the card stock to get the filings to settle over the weaker areas of the magnetic field.

invention, as they were more concerned about installing lighting systems. Moreover, Tesla's six-wire design meant using a lot of copper, which was expensive. Thomas Edison himself always insisted on using the most cost-efficient ways to develop wiring systems, so Tesla's scheme would've most certainly seemed far too pricey to any of Edison's employees.

Yet despite a lack of interest in Tesla's AC talk, Louis Rau, the president of the company, was impressed with his development of an automatic regulator for Edison's dynamos or generators. Therefore, when an expert was needed to solve lighting installation problems at one of the new railroad stations in Strasbourg in the Alsace region in October 1883, Nikola Tesla was chosen to go.

# Strasbourg

During the Franco-Prussian War of 1870–71, the German Empire took control of Strasbourg from France. Then, after the war, the Germans wanted to establish authority and build a strong presence in the city by erecting public buildings, including a central railway station. When the elderly Emperor Wilhelm I visited the new lighting plant at the station for the opening ceremony, a defect in the wiring system nearly caused a catastrophe. When the switch was flipped to turn on the lights, a huge explosion caused a large part of the wall to collapse, and it nearly fell right on top of Wilhelm!

The German government was understandably upset and refused to take the plant. To avoid a huge financial loss, the French-owned Continental Edison Company needed a French-speaking employee to hurry to Alsace to make repairs to the plant's direct current system—and to make peace with the citizens of Strasbourg. Tesla did both.

He quickly pinpointed the flaw in the plant's DC system, but it took him nearly a year to redesign the generators and reinstall the lighting system. By the spring of 1884, the Alsace citizens were satisfied with the repairs, the German government formally accepted the plant, and Tesla was able to return to Paris with "pleasing anticipations," as one of the Continental Edison Company's administrators had promised him "liberal compensation" if he succeeded in Strasbourg.

Unfortunately, Tesla never saw any of the promised reward money. However, while in the Alsace region he did make progress on developing a model for his own AC induction motor. Anticipating an extended stay in Strasbourg, he'd brought along needed supplies and found an after-hours workspace in a mechanical shop near the railroad station. By summer he "finally had the satisfaction of seeing rotation effected [sic] by alternation currents of different phase, and without sliding contacts or commutator" just as he'd pictured in Budapest a year before.

Excited to finally put his vision into existence and operation, Tesla tried to find investors in Strasbourg to help manufacture his AC motors, but nothing panned out. He hoped to find other investors when he returned to Paris, but no one there was interested either. Moreover, after getting the runaround by three company officials, he finally figured out that receiving his bonus for the Strasbourg job was about as likely as being rewarded with "a castle in Spain."

The young inventor was disillusioned by the lack of interest in his motor, and he was upset by the way he'd been treated by his employers. So, when Charles Batchelor urged him to move to America to help redesign Edison machines, the timing was perfect. Tesla was more than ready to try his fortunes in the "Land of Golden Promise."

**Nikola Tesla, when he first arrived in America.** *Tesla Universe*

## America Bound

Two of Tesla's uncles gave him money to help pay for his passage to the United States, and he traveled aboard a steamship named the SS *City of Richmond* for the transatlantic crossing. Unfortunately, he'd discovered that most of his belongings, money, and ticket had been stolen just as he was supposed to board the train leaving Paris. He'd had to run alongside and jump up onto the moving train, but thankfully he'd had enough money in his pocket to pay for a train ticket. But once he reached the port in Liverpool, he'd had to explain his dilemma and wait until no one else claimed his berth before he was allowed to board his ship. Therefore, he arrived in America with very little. Yet, Tesla later claimed that he'd somehow managed to hold onto a letter of introduction from Charles Batchelor to give to Thomas Edison. It said, "I know two great men and you are one of them; the other is this young man."

The 28-year-old Tesla, who'd spent much of his life in cultured and beautiful European cities, initially found New York City to be rough, unattractive, and uncivilized—and at least a century behind the Old World lifestyle he'd enjoyed. But as he left the Castle Garden Immigration Center and made his way through the bustling streets to the home of one of Batchelor's friends where he would stay that night, he had to feel hopeful and excited about the future.

Tesla didn't have money or a job yet, but with his education, training, and specialized skills, he figured he could fare quite well in this New

# WHAT TESLA SAW IN 1884

When Nikola Tesla arrived in his new home of New York City in June 1884, it was the Gilded Age—a term coined by Mark Twain—in America. This simply meant it was a time of great economic growth, yet a period of excessive wealth for only very few. The Gilded Age lasted from the 1870s until about 1900.

In 1884, the Brooklyn Bridge had been completed less than a year before, and Chester Arthur was president of the 38 existing United States. A month after he landed, Tesla would've probably heard that the cornerstone for the Statue of Liberty was laid on Bedloe's Island in New York Harbor. But Tesla didn't see the statue or pass through the Ellis Island immigrant inspection station when he arrived New York because they weren't built yet. Lady Liberty, which was completed in 1886, would become the symbol of hope for a new life for the 12 million other immigrants who later came to America.

Tesla would've most certainly been aware that an earthquake shook New York City and the surrounding areas on August 10. And, in December of that year, he would've probably heard that the Washington Monument had been completed in Washington, DC.

He would've discovered that almost all electrical and lighting systems in America were run by direct current, although inventors were experimenting with alternating current, using it on a smaller and more limited scale.

The young inventor had just arrived in the New World, but significant changes were taking place all around him. It was an age of urbanization and industrialization, and America was stretching and growing. Tesla was ready to make his mark.

# RESEARCH OR REFLECT: WRITE ABOUT AN IMMIGRANT'S EXPERIENCE

Before Ellis Island opened in 1892, a circular sandstone fort named Castle Garden was America's first official immigration center. Nikola Tesla came through the center in 1884 when he was 28 years old. Upon arriving, he might've noticed strange sights, sounds, and smells, and he would've certainly been required to undergo a medical exam before being allowed to leave the processing center. And although Tesla spoke several languages, including English, he probably realized that other immigrants might have trouble with the language barrier.

Perhaps you have a close relative, parent, or grandparent who immigrated to America in the last 50 years—or maybe you were born in another country and recently immigrated to the United States with your family.

For this activity, choose one of the following:

❭ Reflect and write about your own immigration experience.
❭ Interview a family member who immigrated to America and write about his or her experience.
❭ Research and compare a modern immigrant's experience to that of a 19th-century immigrant.

------------------------------------------------------------

## You'll Need

⚡ Library or internet access (optional)

⚡ Paper and pencil, or computer

1. If you choose to reflect and write about your own immigration experience or that of a close relative, use a computer word processing program or simply jot down the stories on a sheet of paper.

2. If you choose to research and compare a modern immigrant's experience to that of a 19th-century immigrant, visit your local library or do online research to read diaries, journals, or books about immigration and immigrants. Online sources to learn more about immigration:

   **Statue of Liberty–Ellis Island Foundation,** www.libertyellisfoundation.org

   **Castle Garden,** www.castlegarden.org

Immigrant Experience in America, www.thirteen.org /edonline/lessons/immigration/index.html

Tenement Museum, www.tenement.org

Recommended books:

*Coming to America: The Story of Immigration* by Betsy Maestro

*If Your Name Was Changed at Ellis Island* by Ellen Levine

*Shutting Out the Sky: Life in the Tenements of New York, 1880-1924* by Deborah Hopkinson

*Ellis Island: An Interactive History Adventure* by Michael Burgan

After your research, write about how a modern immigrant's experience is different or similar to that of a 19th-century immigrant. Consider the impressions, feelings, and fears of both.

World. Moreover, in addition to speaking Serbo-Croatian and English, he was fluent in six other languages: French, German, Czech, Hungarian, Italian, and Latin. In a city overflowing with new immigrants, this ability was a plus. Besides, he was soon to meet with the great Thomas Edison, and he couldn't wait to share his AC system with the one man he was sure would understand the significance of his invention and ideas.

## The Geniuses Meet

Thomas Edison was 37 years old and already world famous when Tesla walked into his lab on South Fifth Avenue that summer day in 1884. According to some historians, it's possible that the two had already met briefly in Paris. But Tesla's recollections focused only on the 1884 meeting in New York, and it's evident that the young Serb was awed by the "Wizard of Menlo Park." He later wrote, "The meeting with Edison was a memorable event in my life. I was amazed at this wonderful man who, without early advantages and scientific training, had accomplished so much."

Edison was not very friendly, nor as impressed by his eager visitor. He was distracted by several crises: an electrical emergency at the Vanderbilt house on Fifth Avenue; a pair of damaged dynamos on the SS *Oregon* (the first boat ever to have electric lighting), which was docked and delayed from sailing; and a leaking junction box at one of his direct current power stations. He probably wasn't in the best mood when Tesla handed him Batchelor's letter. Then again, it may have just been Edison's personality. According to biographer Marc J. Seifer, "Thomas Alva Edison was an extremely complex fellow. Ornery, ingenious, determined, and unyielding."

Whatever the reason, Edison was already skeptical of the foreigner standing in his lab before Tesla ever opened his mouth. But in precise though thickly accented English, Tesla quickly told about the work he'd done for the Continental Edison Company in Paris and Germany, while Edison listened. However, when Tesla launched into a description of his AC induction motor and how much better it was than DC motors, the older inventor became angry and abruptly cut him off. He wouldn't listen to another word. Alternating current was dangerous, and he had no desire to fool with it. Besides, America was set up to use direct current—and that was that!

But Edison still desperately needed an engineer to deal with the lighting issue on the SS *Oregon*, and he figured this pretentious young newcomer would do about as well as any other. If Tesla would forget this AC nonsense, he could have a job with Edison Electric Company. Of course, Tesla was probably disappointed by his reception and Edison's response, but he needed the job. He took his tools and instruments, boarded the vessel, and with the help of the ship's crew, worked all night. Before dawn, he'd repaired the damaged dynamos that powered the ship's lights.

As Tesla was walking back to the lab, he met Edison and a few top employees who'd apparently also worked through the evening and were just going home to rest. It seems Edison made a remark about "our Parisian" running about at night. Was Edison purposely trying to irritate the young Serb by calling him a Parisian or accusing him of carousing at night, rather than working? Who knows. But Tesla quickly informed him that he'd just come from the SS *Oregon*, where he'd successfully finished the task he'd been given. According to Tesla, Edison was surprised and pleased by the answer, and from that time on, Tesla "had full freedom in directing the work."

He regularly worked 18-hour days, seven days a week, helping solve operation and design problems. He also worked with arc lamps, which were used for outdoor street lighting and in large factories. The phenomenon of arc lighting was discovered by Sir Humphry Davy, an English chemist and inventor, in 1802. Davy observed that when two pieces of carbon were connected to a source of high electric voltage, an arc of bright light would strike between them when they were a short distance apart. Over the next 70 years, others used Davy's discovery to develop workable arc lamps. Unfortunately, there were problems with arc lighting, and inventors were always trying to improve upon the system and arc lamp designs.

Tesla's hectic schedule didn't keep him from continuing to think about his AC motor. But he didn't share his ideas with his coworkers or even try to build a new AC motor prototype. He kept quiet and made improvements to his motor only in his mind.

# THOMAS EDISON

Thomas Alva Edison was born on February 11, 1847, in Milan, Ohio, and he grew up in Port Huron, Michigan. He was the youngest of seven children, and he suffered from hearing problems and poor health as a young boy. Because of this, he did not perform well academically, and his teachers claimed he was slow. Therefore, Thomas only attended the local school for a short while before his mother began educating him at home. He read the classics early, and he also taught himself many things.

Despite his nontraditional education, Edison showed remarkable inventive abilities early on. He worked mostly by trial and error and never followed the conventional method of inventing or marketing his creations. Rather, he devised his own way of doing things. He became an apprentice to a telegrapher at age 15 and eventually began working as a telegraph operator. However, he moved around a good bit and lost several jobs because he liked to experiment when he was supposed to be working.

In 1868, Edison received a patent for his first invention, the poorly received electrographic vote recorder. But this device set him on the road to developing more lucrative and successful inventions, including improved telegraph products, the phonograph, incandescent light bulbs, and the earliest motion picture camera. He became known as the Wizard of Menlo Park, the New Jersey town where he lived and worked.

Edison also invested a lot of time and money into creating direct current electrical and lighting systems and power stations, and this ultimately led to many legal and professional battles with others who championed using alternating current. The result was the Current War between Edison and the Westinghouse-Tesla team.

Edison's DC system lost in the Current War, but nonetheless he has been described as America's greatest inventor. With 1,093 patents to his credit, Thomas Edison was a major force in America's industrial and technical growth throughout his lifetime—and in the years since. He died on October 18, 1931, in West Orange, New Jersey.

**Thomas Edison and his early phonograph, circa 1877 or 1878.**
*Brady-Handy Photograph Collection, Prints and Photographs Division, Library of Congress, LC-DIG-cwpbh-04044*

## American Humor?

After he'd been with the company awhile, Tesla announced that he had a plan that could significantly improve the DC generators used to create the electricity in the company's power stations. Always looking for ways to increase efficiency—and profits—Edison jumped at the offer with the remark, "There's fifty thousand dollars in it for you if you can do it."

Tesla worked almost continuously around the clock, and by the spring of 1885, he'd designed or redesigned 24 types of dynamos. Some of these tripled the output of the previous generators without the use of added iron, which was a huge cost consideration. But allegedly, when he asked Edison for his bonus, his employer replied, "Tesla, you don't understand our American humor."

Tesla was outraged. And even though Edison offered him both a $10 raise and a warning that he'd have a tough time finding another engineering job, he quit on the spot and walked out of Edison's office, offended and disgusted—yet still proud and dignified. He was also certain he'd have no trouble finding similar employment elsewhere.

## The Tesla Electric Light and Manufacturing Company

Tesla's reputation as a hard worker and talented inventor had not gone unnoticed by others. Not long after he left Edison's employ, he was approached by two investors who offered to establish the Tesla Electric Light and Manufacturing Company and build him a lab (his first ever) on Grant Street in Rahway, New Jersey. Of course he was interested! He would finally have a chance to develop his alternating current system and present it to the world—or so he thought.

Tesla's investors, Benjamin A. Vail and Robert Lane, had other plans and instead wanted him to develop a better arc lighting lamp design and system before moving on to other projects. So once again, he had to put his AC dreams on hold. But within a year, Tesla had developed a "Tesla arc lamp which was more simple, reliable, safe, and economical than those in current use." Plus, there was "no flickering and hissing." The system was patented in the company's name, and the arc lamps were soon manufactured and put into use.

Tesla was to have been compensated with shares of company stock, but due to the newness of the firm and the condition of the country's economy in early 1886, the "handsomely engraved stock certificate" he received was worth very little money. Moreover, once they had their arc lighting system, Vail and Lane had no further use for Tesla. They certainly had no intention of backing his proposed AC system, so with a bit of manipulation, they forced him out of the very company that bore his name. Furthermore, Tesla was distraught to learn that false rumors were being spread about his abilities as an engineer and inventor.

## Dark Days and Deep Ditches

Betrayed and bankrupt, Tesla "lived through a year of terrible heartaches, [his] suffering being intensified by material want." Desperate for money, he found a job digging ditches for two dollars a day and later claimed that, at that low point in his life, his high education "seemed a mockery." He also "resented the utter waste of his abilities." He rarely talked about these depressing, dark, and hungry days afterward, as the experience was so painful and humiliating for him.

But sometime during the winter of 1887, Tesla must have shared his idea for an induction motor with the foreman of his work crew. This supervisor was very impressed by the young immigrant's accomplishments and plans for an alternating current system, so he introduced Tesla to Alfred S. Brown, manager of the Western Union Telegraph Company. Brown, also an engineer, was knowledgeable and intensely interested in the idea of alternating current, and this meeting proved to be a big turning point in Tesla's career.

## The Deciding Demonstration

Brown then introduced Tesla to a wealthy lawyer (and prospective investor) named Charles Peck, who was initially very skeptical of this business venture. But when Tesla performed an amazing alternating current demonstration called the Egg of Columbus for him, Peck was astonished and convinced of the future role of alternating current in America.

Brown and Peck organized and financed the New York–based Tesla Electric Company, and the men also had a new lab built for Tesla in lower Manhattan, not far from Edison's. He got right to work, and his first goal was to develop and test two full-scale models of the AC induction motor, using the rotating magnetic field, that he'd first envisioned in Budapest.

Eventually, he would also produce three principal polyphase systems, using single-phase, two-phase, and three-phase currents. He also experimented with four- and six-phase currents. For each system, Tesla planned to create dynamos (to generate the electric current), motors (to produce power from the dynamos), transformers (to raise or lower voltages), and all the necessary devices to automatically control the machinery.

Tesla was making $250 a month, but he was working at a frantic pace, sometimes around the clock, with very few breaks. He knew other inventors were also working on similar AC system designs that could certainly "influence the course of history," and he wanted to stay in the lead. Therefore, he was relieved when his talented friend Anthony Szigeti immigrated to America and joined the Tesla team in the spring of 1887.

## Rising Star

The first patent for the Tesla Electric Company was filed on April 30, 1887, marking the beginning of Tesla's successful 15-year inventive streak. (By 1891, he had applied for and received 40 patents.) Within a few months of its launch, the company was already manufacturing and distributing AC induction motors, making Tesla's dream a reality.

More and more people heard about Tesla's alternating current discoveries, and he began

# TESLA'S EGG OF COLUMBUS

There are several versions of the original Egg of Columbus story. But one legend says that Christopher Columbus was mocked by a group of Spanish nobles who claimed that the Americas would've been discovered at some point anyway, and that he had done nothing special.

Upon hearing this, Columbus asked his critics to make an egg stand up on its end. When they could not do it, he gently tapped the egg on the bottom to flatten it, and then he made it stand up. He was making the point that something always looks easy to others—after it's already been done, discovered, or created. It's always harder to be the one who does something new for the first time.

Tesla wanted to impress potential investors with his alternating current know-how. He had the idea and a plan, but he needed to convince the men that investing in him and his future AC motor was a smart idea. He had to show them the potential power of using the rotating magnetic field. Therefore, he came up with his own Egg of Columbus demonstration. A magazine journalist, later recording Tesla's reminiscences of the occasion, stated, "A rotating field magnet was fastened under the top board of a wooden table and [Tesla] provided a copper-plated egg. . . . He placed the egg on the table and to [the associates'] astonishment it stood on end, but when they found it was rapidly spinning their stupefaction was complete."

Thanks to the rotating magnetic field, Tesla's egg spun on its major axis (its base), due to gyroscopic action. The investors were amazed and ready to give Tesla the money he needed to develop his AC motor.

**Tesla's Egg of Columbus demonstration using the rotating magnetic field.** *Tesla Universe*

to gain recognition and accolades—especially from forward-thinking innovators. One of these, Thomas Commerford Martin, editor of *Electrical World* magazine and president of the newly formed American Institute of American Electrical Engineers (AIEE), wanted to persuade Tesla to write an article for his publication and perhaps make a public appearance to discuss his work.

Martin, who would play a significant role in Tesla's life, was "one of the most influential personalities in the glamourous futuristic world of electrical engineering." Moreover, he genuinely liked the "mysterious" and quirky newcomer and was determined to help "choreograph Tesla's entrée into the electrical-engineering community." Therefore, his first job as self-appointed publicist was to coax Tesla into agreeing to present his induction motor before the AIEE.

The presentation was scheduled for May 16, 1888, but Tesla was still reluctant to fully share about his work. In fact, it was only on the night before his lecture that he finally penciled out his now-classic address entitled "A New System of Alternating Current Motors and Transformers." Much to his surprise, he discovered he enjoyed lecturing to the large crowd the next day. And he was good at it! His explanation of how alternating current could be generated and sent over long distances to power his induction motor was so simple that even attendees with limited knowledge of the subject could understand it. He also easily described how his transformers could "step up" or "step down" voltage to be useful. And he had all the patents to prove he'd created the system he now shared.

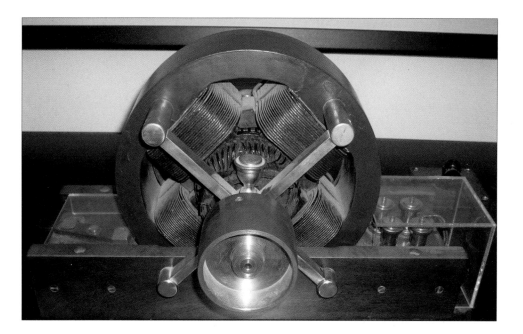

**Tesla's AC induction motor.**
*Wikimedia Commons*

According to biographer John J. O'Neill, "Tesla's lecture, and the inventions and discoveries which he included in it, established him before the electrical engineering profession as the father of the whole field of alternating-current power system, and the outstanding inventor in the electrical field."

Another famous gentleman was also interested in what Tesla had to say—as well as his patents. He'd been working with alternating current to power lighting systems for some time, but he was still missing some of the pieces of the puzzle. It seemed that Tesla and his patents might just be the answer to his problem. Therefore, it wasn't long before Tesla received an invitation to meet with this well-known American industrial giant and inventor to discuss a partnership. The man's name was George Westinghouse.

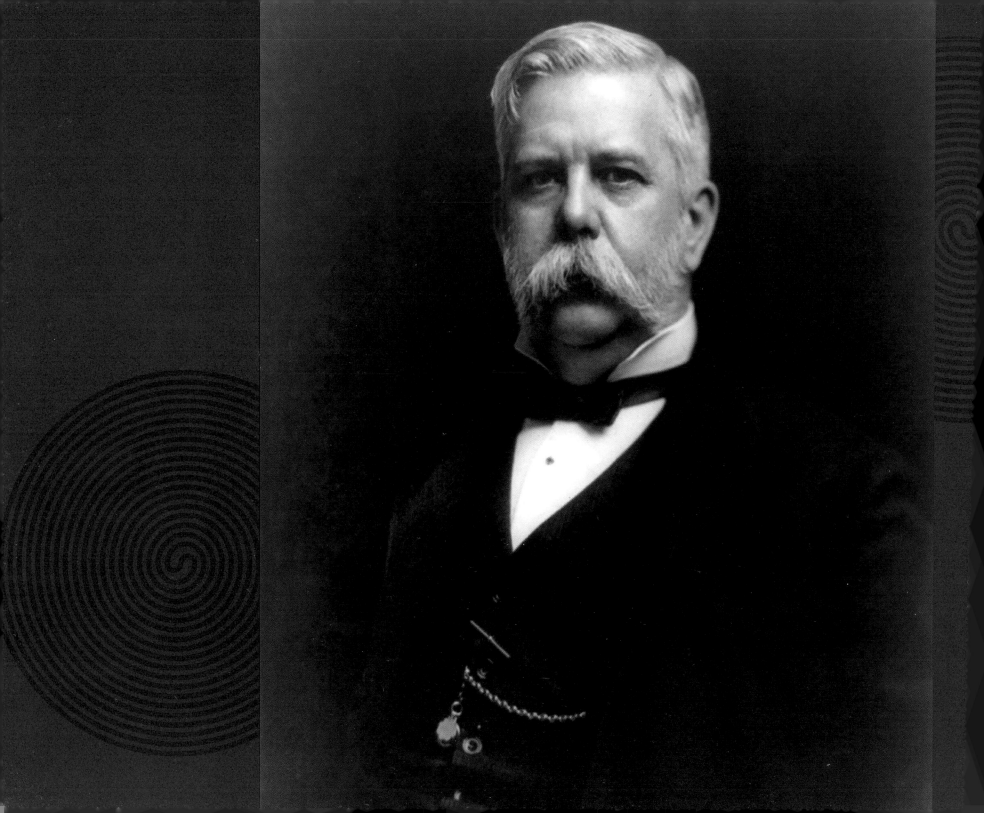

# ROADBLOCKS AND VICTORIES

*The scientific man does not aim at an immediate result. He does not expect that his advanced ideas will be readily taken up. His work is like that of a planter—for the future. His duty is to lay foundation for those who are to come and point the way.* —Nikola Tesla

George Westinghouse was a man who knew what he wanted, and he was accustomed to getting it. By the time he met Tesla in early 1888, the decade-older Westinghouse was already a successful American entrepreneur and inventor. He'd developed and patented the railway air brake while still in his early 20s, and later he made improvements to railroad signaling systems as well.

**George Westinghouse, circa early 1900s.** *Prints and Photographs Division, Library of Congress, LC-USZ62-93492*

# GEORGE WESTINGHOUSE

George Westinghouse was born on October 6, 1846, in New York and grew up in Pittsburgh, Pennsylvania. His family was not wealthy, and George was the eighth of ten children. Like many other famous inventors and scientists, he was considered slow and never did well academically. He quit school at the age of 14 and went to work for his father, who ran a machine shop. However, like Thomas Edison, George showed a natural aptitude for inventing and creating at a very early age.

He was 15 years old when the Civil War began, and he ran away to join the New York National Guard. His parents made him return home, but a year later, he convinced them to let him rejoin. He served in both the Union army and navy. Afterward, he attended college for a while, but found that institutional learning was not for him. He dropped out and began his long and successful career as an inventor, industrialist, and entrepreneur, gaining his first patent at age 19.

Undoubtedly, Westinghouse's most famous invention was his air brake system, but he held over 300 patents during his lifetime. He was also known as a fair employer who treated his workers well. In fact, Westinghouse's company was the first to initiate 9-hour work days, 55-hour work weeks, and half days on Saturdays. These may seem to be long work hours by today's standards, but in those days most employers expected their employees to work 12 to 16 hours a day, seven days a week. Therefore, Westinghouse's reduced work hours and work week policies were extremely unusual for the times.

George married his wife, Marguerite, in 1867, and they had one son. Westinghouse died in 1914. As a Civil War veteran, he was given the honor of being buried in Arlington National Cemetery in Washington, DC.

Moreover, Westinghouse was a pioneer in the electrical industry and famous for inventing and patenting numerous other electrical devices. He ultimately made a fortune manufacturing and marketing his own inventions, but he was also a savvy businessman and regularly bought invention patents held by others if he thought they would be profitable or if they might be used by competitors to block him later on.

Although Westinghouse, like Edison, utilized and built direct current generating stations on a smaller scale for his Pittsburgh-based Westinghouse Electric Company (to power residential lighting systems), he'd also been one of the first to see the commercial potential for alternating current several years before Tesla ever immigrated to America. He knew that Thomas Edison's company was financially limited to serving customers in densely populated areas who lived close enough to one of his power stations. Therefore, there was a big market to light up less populated towns and cities that were out of Edison's reach. Westinghouse was determined to capitalize on this.

Westinghouse realized that alternating current could be generated and transmitted long distances without losing energy, but he also knew that he would need some way to reduce or "step down" the dangerously high voltage before it could safely enter people's homes to power the AC-compatible incandescent lights. He just needed all the parts to make this new business venture work.

He asked his head engineer, William Stanley Jr., to design an AC incandescent lighting system. He sent another associate to Europe in 1885 to pay $50,000 for the rights to the patents of an AC transformer system that had been developed by the French and English team of Lucien Gaulard and John Dixon Gibbs. Everything seemed to be on track, and the Westinghouse Electric Company began operating its first commercial AC system in Buffalo, New York, in 1886.

# A New Partnership

Westinghouse's engineers soon discovered the system had problems, and it was difficult to build an efficient transformer. Moreover, there still wasn't a practical alternating current motor available (that didn't use a commutator), and Westinghouse knew that a serviceable AC motor could be the selling point for prospective buyers. Therefore, when he heard about Tesla's complete alternating current system, he knew he'd finally found the missing pieces to his own AC puzzle.

From their very first meeting, Tesla and Westinghouse had a good working relationship based on mutual respect. And when Westinghouse offered to buy the patents for his AC Polyphase System, Tesla didn't hesitate. There are varying accounts regarding the sale of the patents, but according to biographer W. Bernard Carlson, Tesla received $25,000 in cash, $50,000 in stock certificates, and an agreement to earn $2.50 royalty per horsepower for each motor. In time, these royalties could add up to an extraordinary amount of money. Tesla also agreed to move to Pittsburgh for one year to become a Westinghouse consultant for a salary of $2,000 per month.

## The Pittsburgh Period

Tesla's transition to Pittsburgh was not completely worry-free for the young inventor. For one thing, as a newly celebrated inventor, he'd just started receiving invitations from New York's super-rich citizens, and Tesla enjoyed their attention. For his whole life, he would appreciate elegance and fine dining, and he was hesitant to leave the elite social circles he'd just been allowed to enter.

And when Tesla did arrive at the Westinghouse Electric Company in July 1888, he found that his European-styled induction motor, which was based on the use of low frequency current of 60 cycles, was not exactly compatible with the 133-cycle current used in the existing Westinghouse power plants. In fact, there was no standardized frequency of electric current at all in the United States at that time. The Westinghouse engineers had no desire to change anything on their end, so they tried for quite some time to make Tesla's motor work on their standard. He informed them that they were wrong, which irritated them. Eventually, however, the Westinghouse Electric Company adopted a 60-cyle standard, which Tesla demanded, and then everything worked perfectly.

Satisfied he'd done his job, and restless to return to New York and his new lab on Grand Street, Tesla left Pittsburgh in August 1889. Then, in September, he traveled to Paris to attend the International Exposition and continued to Croatia afterward to visit his mother and sisters. This was the first time he'd returned to Europe since immigrating to America five years earlier, and it was a much-needed break—especially since he'd soon be facing some vicious electrical battles when he returned to New York.

## The War of the Currents Begins

Thomas Edison and George Westinghouse were already enemies; they'd been wrapped up in legal battles for several years. Therefore, the successful Westinghouse-Tesla partnership angered Edison even more.

According to one of Edison's biographers, "There is no doubt that Edison was swayed by passion and hatred for Westinghouse, whom he considered no better than a thief entering a private domain. Rage consumed this man of moods. All the hatred of which he was so capable extended to Tesla and the entire alternating current forces."

Edison also realized that if AC systems continued to gain popularity, they could destroy the DC empire he'd been building for years. He needed a way to discredit this entire alternating current business and the men behind it. So, although an industrial battle to control the standard of electricity in America had been threatening for some time, the partnership of Westinghouse and Tesla caused it to erupt into full-fledged combat—the War of the Currents.

Thomas Edison used propaganda and fear tactics to convince the public that alternating current was dangerous, and he hired an electrical engineer named Harold Pitney Brown to help him. Brown was outspoken and seemed to thrive on electrical current debates and drama. He'd even

# THE EXPOSITION UNIVERSELLE OF 1889

The Exposition Universelle, or Paris Exposition of 1889, was a world's fair held on the Champ de Mars from May 6 to October 31, 1889. Although other countries, including the United States, had exhibitions, the international fair was actually a 100th anniversary celebration of the storming of the Bastille at the beginning of the French Revolution in 1789.

The main attraction was the Eiffel Tower, the 984-foot tall iron structure, designed and built for the exhibition by Gustave Eiffel's company. The bottom archways of the "iron lady" served as the entrance to the fair. At night, the structure was lit by hundreds of gas lamps, and a beacon flashed three beams of red, white, and blue lights. Two tower searchlights illuminated the grounds after dark for evening guests, and booms from a cannon at the top signaled the opening and closing times of the fair each day. The Eiffel Tower was only meant to be a temporary structure in Paris, and it was almost torn down in 1909. But city officials realized the iconic structure was a valuable tourist attraction, and it is still the most visited paid monument in the world today.

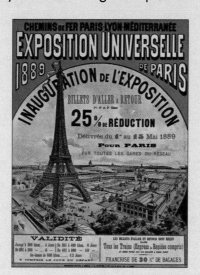

Many famous people visited or participated in the Paris Exposition during the six months it operated, including Buffalo Bill and Annie Oakley with the Wild West Show; the future English king Edward VII and his wife, Alexandra; composer Claude Debussy; artists Vincent van Gogh and James Abbott McNeill Whistler; and author Henry James. Both Nikola Tesla and Thomas Edison attended as well, and Edison was thrilled by the public recognition, attention, and praise he received while there.

The Paris Exposition of 1889 was highly successful and profitable, and it set a high mark for America to follow when plans began to be made for the Columbian Exposition, or the Chicago's World Fair of 1893, not long after the exposition in Paris ended.

**A poster for the Paris Exposition of 1889.**
*Wikimedia Commons*

electrocuted animals to demonstrate to an 1886 New York research committee that death by electrocution (rather than hanging) was the quickest and most humane method of capital punishment for convicted murderers. Although there had been accidental deaths attributed to direct current electrocution, Brown believed that AC was far more dangerous—and therefore it should be the chosen death current. He was the perfect man to help Edison win the war.

A postcard showing the many criss-crossed overhead telegraph, telephone, and power lines along Broadway Street, in New York City, circa 1885–87.
*Prints and Photographs Division, Library of Congress, LC-DIG-pga-00028*

In Edison's defense, he truly did believe that direct current was much safer than alternating current, but his means of trying to prove himself right were extreme. He allowed Brown to come to his Menlo Park lab in December 1888 and publicly perform gruesome animal electrocutions to demonstrate the deadly powers of alternating current. It was also about this time that families in the West Orange, New Jersey, area noticed a pattern of disappearing pets. It was later rumored that Edison paid local schoolboys 25 cents for each cat or dog they brought in for experiments.

Edison and Brown also exploited all the human deaths by accidental electrocution they heard about and even fabricated stories about AC tragedies to alarm citizens. As biographer Margaret Cheney noted, "As Edison saw it, accidents caused by AC must, if they could not be found, be manufactured, and the public alerted to the hazards. Not only were fortunes at stake in the War of the Currents but also the personal pride of an egocentric genius."

Brown soon came up with an even better publicity idea. Why not secretly purchase and use some of Westinghouse's own motors to use in their demonstrations and work? He could fuel the public's fear by allowing people to see what destruction and death could be caused by these specific AC-producing dynamos!

First, Brown experimented by electrocuting larger animals, including two calves and a horse. Edison began to refer to deaths by electrocution as being "Westinghoused!" Of course, Westinghouse was justifiably upset by the term and the exhibitions, as he felt they were inhumane and a source of bad publicity. But then Brown took it a step further. When the New York prison commission finally voted in June 1888 to replace death by hanging with death by electrocution to punish convicted murderers, he created the electric chair that would be used to perform the very first electrical execution—and the design would use a Westinghouse motor to generate the alternating current.

The convicted killer sentenced to die in the electric chair was 30-year-old William Kemmler, who had murdered his common-law wife with a hatchet on March 29, 1888. The execution did not take place until August 6, 1890, at Auburn Prison in New York. Unfortunately for Kemmler, it did not go as planned. The first surge of more than 1,000 volts was applied for 17 seconds to Kemmler in the chair. He was pronounced dead—until a spectator saw him still breathing. The voltage was obviously too low, so attendants quickly switched the dynamo up to full power for almost two more minutes. But the gruesome sight and torturous sounds of the following moments were revolting to those who watched. Many got sick or rushed out as "the stench of burning flesh filled the room."

The botched execution was a nightmare. Brown and Edison's claim that just a small amount of alternating current could easily kill a man was questioned, because Kemmler's death was neither quick nor painless. In fact, one doctor who was present claimed he'd have rather seen "ten hangings than such execution as this." Tesla must have agreed, because 40 years later he said that those who were executed by early electrocution methods were "literally roasted alive." And as for H. P. Brown, he disappeared from public sight, never to be heard from again.

## Wireless Power Discoveries

After selling his patents to Westinghouse, Tesla's fortunes changed considerably. When he first returned to New York from Pittsburgh, he'd moved into the Astor House in downtown Manhattan, a five-story hotel known for its style and grandeur. This move began his pattern of exclusive hotel living that lasted the rest of his life. He also began to dine more often at New York's finest restaurants, such as Delmonico's, where he enjoyed socializing with friends—many of them extremely famous and wealthy.

Yet, while the events of the Current War swirled about him, Tesla stayed busy. He moved into a new lab on South Fifth Avenue, which took up the entire fourth floor of a six-story building. And here, in his much bigger space, he began experimenting with ideas such as high-frequency alternating current, wireless transmission, electromagnetic energy, and even X-rays. This work was the beginning of his lifelong quest to provide free and unlimited wireless energy to the world. It has even been suggested by some historians that his motivation was also fueled by his early conservationist concern for the earth's limited natural resources of timber and coal.

Scientists had known for some time that visible light was one form of electromagnetic

# TESLA'S FAMOUS FRIENDS

T. C. Martin, publisher of *Electrical World* magazine, was serious about his mission to promote Tesla's work, but he also introduced the inventor to an influential New York couple who greatly impacted his life. Through them, Tesla would connect with wealthy society people and well-known writers, performers, artists, scientists, and naturalists of the day.

Tesla met Robert Underwood Johnson, associate editor (later the editor in chief) of the *Century* magazine, and his wife, Katharine, in 1894, and a deep friendship developed that lasted the rest of their lives. Tesla spent a lot of time at the Johnsons' home, and he usually enjoyed the holidays with them as well.

Robert was prominent in political, literary, and social circles. He championed forestry conservation, preservation of natural landmarks, and children's causes, and he was well known for his work with international copyright law.

Katharine was especially close to Tesla, and she took a special interest in his personal life and relationships with others. The two were strictly friends, but some historians think that Tesla might have loved Katharine and considered her to be an ideal woman to whom no one else could ever measure up. Others disagree with that idea, but it's undeniable that Tesla admired Katharine Johnson and had great affection for her.

The Johnsons introduced Tesla to the Scottish American naturalist and poet John Muir, who is known as the "Father of National Parks." His efforts helped establish Yosemite, Grand Canyon, Kings Canyon, Petrified Forest, and Mount Rainier National Parks, as well as the Sierra Club. His writings also influenced other conservation efforts all over the United States. He admired Tesla for trying to use renewable energy for his inventions and minimize the destruction of natural resources.

Mark Twain had become one of Tesla's closest friends, and the inventor could also boast friendships (made through the Johnsons) with Polish pianist Ignacy Jan Paderewski, British author of *The Jungle Book* Rudyard Kipling, children's author Mary Mapes Dodge, sculptor Augustus Saint-Gaudens, celebrated architect Stanford White, Czech composer Antonín Leopold Dvořák, Spanish-American War hero Richmond P. Hobson, actress Sarah Bernhardt, and railroad heir William "Willie K." Vanderbilt, to name a few.

For a man who would become a social recluse in his later years, Tesla enjoyed being "something of a society darling, a sought-after guest swirling through Manhattan's most glittering homes, private salons, and lavish restaurants." In return, he hosted elaborate dinner parties in private rooms at Delmonico's. This was the golden age of Nikola Tesla's life.

radiation—electricity that vibrates (or travels in the shape of invisible waves) at a very high fre-

...etic radiation ...aves, gamma ...and infrared ...s. Frequency ... the alternat- ...ack-and-forth

...crease electri- ...al to those of ...ant light that ...is might even ...ient incandes- ...t energy pro- ...ess dangerous ...mlessly across ...going into the ...

...a device that ...cies failed, as ...bout the room ...But he finally ...ction coils and ...extremely pre- ...He patented it ...ansformer, but it soon became known as the Tesla coil. This basic design of a spark coil attached to a capacitor—a device that stores an electric charge—operating at a specific frequency is still the foundation of all wireless transmission.

While experimenting with high-frequency currents in November 1890, Tesla had also discovered

Tesla's oscillating transformer, or Tesla coil, created electricity with high frequencies and voltages.
*Wikimedia Commons*

that this electricity could travel through the air and light up a sealed glass bulb filled with gases inside, as well as electrodeless vacuum tubes. He hung a coil wire from the ceiling in his lab, then stood in the middle of the room with vacuum tubes in each hand. When an assistant flipped on the transformer's switch and the cordless and wireless tubes lit up like flaming swords of light in

# MAKE A PATENT DRAWING

A patent is a grant or license from the government that gives an inventor the exclusive right to manufacture, use, or sell the invention for a certain amount of time. An inventor must apply for a patent, supplying invention details and usually a drawing. Once government officials make sure the work is original and grant the patent, the invention is given a special number.

Some inventions are practical, and their patent drawings are recognizable. But some older patent drawings may look silly to us today.

Now it's your turn to create a patent drawing.

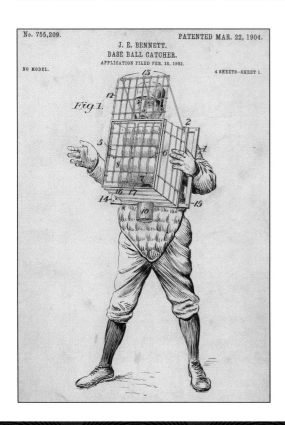

A 1903 patent drawing for a "base ball catcher." *Wikimedia Commons*

## You'll Need

⚡ Computer with internet access

⚡ Paper and pencil

⚡ Art supplies (optional)

1. Explore the United States Patent and Trademark Office website's page for kids at www.uspto.gov /kids/kids.html. Read about how inventors apply for and receive patents.

2. Brainstorm an idea for a cool invention you'd like to "patent." Make it as quirky or practical as you wish.

3. Write a brief description of the invention, then create a patent drawing similar to those on this page. Be sure to include your name, file date, and the title of your invention. Assign yourself a patent number to add to your drawing. Who knows? One day, you and your invention could become world famous.

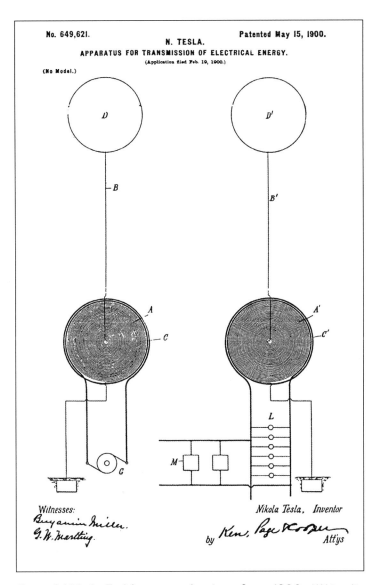

No. 649,621. Patented May 15, 1900.
N. TESLA.
APPARATUS FOR TRANSMISSION OF ELECTRICAL ENERGY.
(Application filed Feb. 19, 1900.)
(No Model.)

Witnesses:
Benjamin Miller.
G. W. Martling.

Nikola Tesla, Inventor
by Ken, Page & Cooper
Attys

**One of Nikola Tesla's patent drawings from 1900.** *Wikimedia Commons*

his hands, Tesla knew for sure that he had transmitted wireless energy through the air. Fluorescent illumination would become one of his most spectacular demonstrations during lectures and presentations. He also later used the same principle to light up glass tubes filled with gas to create the first colorful neon lights.

**Tesla was called the "New Wizard of the West" in the May 1899 issue of *Pearson's Magazine*. The article was accompanied by this illustration of Tesla in his lab holding "balls of flame."** *University of California, Berkeley, Library*

# MIX FLUORESCENT SLIME

*Early in his career, one of Tesla's most popular demonstrations was fluorescent illumination. Later, he would use the same principle to create neon lights. In this activity, you too can create a fluorescent product using just three simple ingredients.*

## You'll Need

⚡ Liquid starch

⚡ Disposable bowl or cup

⚡ Small bottle of glow-in-the-dark acrylic paint

⚡ Plastic spoon or craft stick

⚡ Clear school glue

⚡ Paper towels

1. Pour about ¼ cup (60 milliliters) of the liquid starch into a disposable bowl or cup.

2. Add 1–2 tablespoons (15–30 milliliters) of glow-in-the-dark paint to the starch and stir well with a disposable spoon or craft stick.

3. Stir in ¼ cup (60 milliliters) of clear school glue and mix well for 1 or 2 minutes. The slimy mixture should become very thick.

4. Place the slime mixture on paper towels and blot dry. There may be a bit of liquid still left over in the mixing container—it can be thrown in the trash.

5. Stretch and squeeze the slime mixture until it's smooth and pliable. Turn out the lights. Does your slime glow?

LIQUID STARCH

Glow-in-the-Dark ACRYLIC PAINT

—clear— SCHOOL GLUE

## Forfeiting Untold Wealth

A commercial depression struck the United States in 1890, and Westinghouse was feeling the financial effects. Westinghouse's company had expanded a great deal after buying Tesla's patents, and now he was having money troubles. It was also a time of business mergers and reorganization of companies, and Westinghouse Electric was consolidating with two other companies.

One of the requirements of the merger, however, was that Westinghouse would have to drop some of his projects. Financial advisors told him that his royalty contract with Tesla could jeopardize the newly merged company's ability to succeed or even stay afloat. Doing away with Tesla's royalty agreements was the only way save the company. Westinghouse strongly objected, as he had a powerful sense of justice, but the advisors were stubborn. Something had to be done immediately.

Westinghouse was embarrassed, but he "never hesitated to face facts squarely and with blunt directness." So, he went to visit Tesla in his lab and explained the situation. When he heard of Westinghouse's dilemma and that his (Tesla's) decision could determine the fate of the company, he didn't hesitate—just as he hadn't hesitated four years earlier when Westinghouse offered to buy the patents to his polyphase system. A promise that his polyphase system would continue to be developed and shared with others was enough for Tesla.

He thanked Westinghouse for being his friend and believing in him and supporting him when no one else would. Then he tore the royalties contract into pieces. This one decision likely cost Nikola Tesla millions of dollars that could have saved him from poverty in his later years, but he was never bitter toward Westinghouse. Indeed, in a 1938 speech, he said, "George Westinghouse was, in my opinion, the only man on this globe who could take my alternating-current system under the circumstances then existing and win the battle against prejudice and money power. He was a pioneer of imposing stature, one of the world's true noblemen of whom America may well be proud and to whom humanity owes an immense debt of gratitude."

As it happened, George Westinghouse would not be the only inventor affected by the economic crisis. In 1892, stockholders in Thomas Edison's company, led by John Pierpont (J. P.) Morgan Sr., would make the decision to merge with the Thomson-Houston Electric Company to create the General Electric Company. Edison's name would no longer be used, and he would have no control over the company's decisions.

## Lectures, Citizenship, and Sadness

People began to wonder about the strange lights, sounds, and goings-on in Tesla's lab. In addition, Tesla's good friend T. C. Martin had previously written a full-page article about him in *Electrical World*, so public interest in the Serbian inventor and his work was at an all-time high in the early 1890s.

Tesla finally agreed to give another lecture before the American Institute of Electrical Engineers at New York's Columbia University to discuss his latest discoveries and inventions. On May 20, 1891, he presented "Experiments with Alternate Currents of Very High Frequency and Their Application to Methods of Artificial Illumination." He showed the attending scientists and engineers his oscillators, new bulbs, vacuum tubes, and fluorescent and neon lights.

The title of Tesla's three-hour lecture might have sounded dull; his appearance, though, was anything but. He sported white tie and tails, and his special cork-soled shoes made him almost seven feet tall. He appeared as a "weird, storklike figure on the lecture platform" as he performed groundbreaking demonstrations that amazed his audience, especially when he touched the terminal of a high-frequency oscillator that generated tens of thousands of volts with one hand and illuminated a bulb held in his other hand. There were no cords or wires anywhere. It was like magic, but as Tesla had already discovered, it was simply the "skin effect" of high-frequency voltages passing across the body, rather than going through it.

He informed his audience that he'd only selected observations that he thought would most likely interest them, but that the field was still wide open to research and discovery. He also pointed out, "We are whirling through endless space with inconceivable speed, all around us everything is spinning, everything is moving, everywhere is energy."

Tesla also celebrated another milestone in 1891. On June 21, the Ames Power Plant opened in the little mining town of Telluride, Colorado. It was the first power station to use his AC system to transmit electricity over a long distance and furnish light to outlying mining camps. But perhaps the greatest highlight of his year was becoming an American citizen on July 30, 1891. Nikola Tesla was said to have valued his citizenship more than any scientific honor he ever received.

Over the next year, Tesla would travel to London, Paris, Zagreb, and Belgrade to give more spellbinding lectures like his Columbia University presentation, making him one of the world's most celebrated scientists and changing his private life forever. Unfortunately, during the first part of his Paris lecture, he got word from his uncle that his mother's health was failing. He quickly made his way to Croatia, where Đuka died on April 4, 1892.

Devastated by his loss and falling ill himself (possibly from the stress), Tesla stayed on in Gospić for six more weeks to mourn and recuperate and spend time with his sisters before continuing his scheduled lecture tour. When he returned to New York in September 1892, he moved from the Astor House into the more modern Gerlach Hotel near Madison Square Garden. And although the divisive War of the Currents had continued while Tesla was away, it would soon be settled decisively.

## Lighting the White City

George Westinghouse had been eyeing the contract for a future hydropower station at Niagara Falls, New York, for some time, but the International Niagara Commission chairman, Sir

William Thomson (Lord Kelvin), and the other investors, including J. P. Morgan, John Jacob Astor IV, and W. K. Vanderbilt, were unconvinced that alternating current was safe. The project was still undecided, so Westinghouse turned his attention in a different direction.

Plans had been in the works for years to commemorate and celebrate the 400th anniversary of Christopher Columbus's 1492 voyage to America. And although the opening of the Columbian Exposition (also known as the Chicago World's Fair) was delayed until May 1893 because of the 1892 presidential election, it was an exciting time for all Americans—and especially for those living in Chicago, Illinois, where it would be held.

The exhibition was to last for six months, and the highlight of the event was to be the illumination of thousands of bulbs to light up the buildings and fairgrounds at night. To surpass Paris's 1891 International Exposition, American organizers needed something big, and this first ever all-electric fair promised to be spectacular. Moreover, it would help take American minds off the financial and political troubles plaguing the nation.

Electric companies were invited to submit bids for the fair's lighting contract, and the big question was whether the exposition would be powered by AC or DC. General Electric (planning to use Edison's DC technology) initially bid $1.8 million but later lowered it to $544,000. Westinghouse (planning to use Tesla's AC polyphase system) underbid GE and won the contract at $399,000.

Westinghouse and Tesla were thrilled, but with the lower bid they would now have to create a more economical design to hopefully break even. But in the end, they figured the publicity would outweigh any sum of money made. And a success at the fair might just decide who ultimately won the Niagara Falls contract. This was probably a good attitude, because they immediately ran into a big problem: Edison, angry because his system wouldn't be used, refused to give Westinghouse a license to produce and use Edison's standard light bulb design, to which he held the patent. Undeterred, Westinghouse had his engineers quickly modify and produce 250,000 "stopper lamps" to use instead.

On Monday, May 1, 1893, President Grover Cleveland gave the fair's opening speech, and then, as a choir burst into the "Hallelujah" chorus, he pressed a gold-and-ivory telegraph key to bring a 2,000-horsepower steam engine to life in Machinery Hall. This machine then powered up the 12 Westinghouse generators, each weighing 75 tons, and electricity began to pulse through the wires around the grounds—thanks to Tesla's amazing AC polyphase system design. According to historian Jill Jonnes, "All told, twenty-seven million visitors (half Americans, half foreigners) would pay fifty cents to enter the great fair and experience its astonishments. Above all else, visitors came to marvel at the fair's electrical astonishments."

The Columbian Exposition was an astounding success. Just as Westinghouse and Tesla had hoped, the event introduced the age of electricity—and specifically alternating current electricity—to fairgoers on a grand scale. No longer would the American public be satisfied with anything less

# "VISIT" THE 1893 WORLD'S COLUMBIAN EXPOSITION

*The World's Columbian Exposition of 1893 showed visitors the possibilities of a modern era in America. There were new inventions, consumer products, art, architecture, exhibits, and displays. There were even replicas of iconic American symbols, including a Statue of Liberty made of salt and a Brooklyn Bridge made of soap. Most states and many countries had buildings or displays, and fairgoers were mesmerized by foreign culture exhibits, demonstrations, and entertainment.*

*Explore the Columbian Exposition of 1893 by creating a display or PowerPoint presentation.*

## You'll Need

⚡ Library or internet access

⚡ Poster board, pens and markers, scissors, glue, and art supplies (or computer with PowerPoint)

1. Choose one of following topics—or come up with one of your own.

   ❱ Planning and Construction of the Exposition

   ❱ New Consumer Products

   ❱ Amusement and Entertainment

   ❱ Inventions and Technology

   ❱ State Buildings

   ❱ International Exhibits

   ❱ Art and Architecture

   ❱ Famous People of the Fair

   ❱ Strange Occurrences or Incidents

2. Do online research or read books and articles about the fair. Some good online sources to learn more about the World's Columbian Exposition are:

   **American Historama,** www.american-historama.org/1881-1913-maturation-era/chicago-world-fair.htm

   **The World's Fair, Chicago 1893,** https://worldsfairchicago1893.com

   **Kiddle Encyclopedia, World's Columbian Exposition,** https://kids.kiddle.co/World%27s_Columbian_Exposition

   **Library of Congress** (search images or newspapers), www.loc.gov

than an electrically illuminated world. And that demand would have to be met by building new power generation plants that could transmit electricity to homes both near and far. This included hydropower plants, such as the one that was to be built at Niagara Falls.

**University of Chicago Library,** http://ecuip.lib.uchicago.edu/diglib/social/worldsfair_1893/index.html

**Illinois Institute of Technology,** http://columbus.iit.edu/index.html

**Some recommended books are:**

*The Chicago World's Fair of 1893: A Photographic Record* by Stanley Appelbaum

*The World's Columbian Exposition: The Chicago World's Fair of 1893* by Norman Bolotin and Christine Laing

*Chicago History for Kids: Triumphs and Tragedies of the Windy City, with 21 Activities* by Owen Hurd

*Mr. Ferris and His Wheel* by Kathryn Gibbs Davis

3. After your research, create a poster board display or make a PowerPoint presentation to share with classmates, family members, or friends.

# THE WORLD'S COLUMBIAN EXPOSITION OF 1893

The fair put America in the international spotlight. It also put Chicago on the map in a big way, as it had beaten out New York City, Washington, DC, and St. Louis to win the honor of host city. Chicago architect Daniel H. Burnham headed up the talented team of designers and architects who would develop the fair site and buildings at Jackson Park, an area along the shore of Lake Michigan. He also engaged famed American landscape architecture Frederick Law Olmsted to help design the grounds.

**Court of Honor, Columbian Exposition, 1893.** *By C. D. Arnold (1844–1927); H. D. Higinbotham, Wikimedia Commons*

A large, rectangular water pool represented Columbus's long sea voyage. This Grand Basin was surrounded by ornate white buildings and pavilions. A large figure called the Statue of the Republic stood at one end in the Court of Honor.

There were many exciting things for fairgoers to see, including international exhibits and buildings, state buildings, life-sized replicas of Columbus's three ships, technology displays, the first commercial movie theater, a moving sidewalk called a travelator, and boat rides. Visitors were also introduced to Cracker Jack, Juicy Fruit gum, Quaker Oats, and shredded wheat for the very first time.

There were carnival sideshows and rides in a separate area called the Midway. The top attraction was the new 264-foot tall Ferris Wheel, built by George Washington Gale Ferris Jr., Chicago's answer to Paris's Eiffel Tower.

The Electrical Building was the most important place on the fairgrounds to Tesla, as the Westinghouse Company displayed several polyphase systems there. One section showcased Tesla's electrical inventions and devices, including his two-phase induction motor, generators, transformers, Tesla coil, Egg of Columbus, phosphorescent lighting, neon signs, and more. The fair gave his AC polyphase system a platform for international exposure.

The fair was successful—both culturally and financially. It was a turning point for America as the country began to head into a modern era.

**The original Ferris Wheel could hold 2,160 people.** *Wikimedia Commons*

**The Electrical Building, Chicago World's Fair, 1893.** *Tesla Universe*

# FROM WATERFALLS TO WARDENCLYFFE

*My paramount desire today, which guides me in everything I do, is an ambition to harness the forces of nature for the service of mankind.* —Nikola Tesla

Lord Kelvin had been a very strong opponent of using alternating current at the Niagara Falls hydroelectric power station, and he'd urged the advisory committee to avoid it at all costs. But after he visited the Columbian Exposition and saw Tesla's AC demonstrations, he completely changed his mind. George Westinghouse and Nikola Tesla had successfully proven alternating current to be superior and more cost effective, especially for transmitting electricity over longer distances.

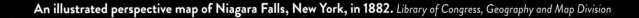

**An illustrated perspective map of Niagara Falls, New York, in 1882.** *Library of Congress, Geography and Map Division*

SCIENTIFIC AMERICAN

[Entered at the Post Office of New York, N.Y., as Second Class matter. Copyright, 1896, by Munn & Co.]

A WEEKLY JOURNAL OF PRACTICAL INFORMATION, ART, SCIENCE, MECHANICS, CHEMISTRY, AND MANUFACTURES.

Vol. LXXIV.—No. 4.
Established 1845.

NEW YORK, JANUARY 25, 1896.

[$3.00 A YEAR.
Weekly.

THE POWER CANAL AND BUILDINGS.

INTERIOR OF THE CABLE BRIDGE.

OILING AND COOLING PIPES.

THE DYNAMOS.

THE FRICTION BRAKE.

**The Niagara Falls Power Plant was featured in** *Scientific American* **magazine on January 25, 1896.** *Author's collection*

In October 1893, the International Niagara Commission advised Edward Dean Adams, president of the Cataract Construction Company, to award Westinghouse and Tesla the contract to build the powerhouse and generators to harness the force of the falls to produce electricity. As a compromise, Adams awarded General Electric the contract to build the transmission and distribution lines from Niagara Falls to Buffalo, New York.

Westinghouse's powerhouse at the falls was finished by 1895. The first large generator, bearing Tesla's name and patent numbers, was successfully tested on April 15, 1895, and General Electric completed the transmission and distribution lines the following year. On November 16, 1896, the switch was thrown at the Niagara Falls hydroelectric power plant. Within seconds, electricity powered up the lights and streetcars in Buffalo, which was 26 miles away.

The War of the Currents was permanently settled "with a victory for Tesla's system of AC and Westinghouse's perseverance." Within a few years, more generators were added to the plant, which would become known as the Adams Power Station, and Niagara Falls would eventually provide electricity to New York City, about 400 miles away. When Tesla, along with George Westinghouse, toured the soon-to-open station filled with equipment operating on his AC system for the first time in July 1896, he must have recalled his boyhood dream of harnessing the mighty waters of Niagara Falls to produce energy on a grand scale. That dream was now a reality.

# BUILD A WATERWHEEL

*Today, most electricity generated by hydropower comes from hydroelectric dams. But for generations, waterwheels were used as a source of power—especially for grinding grain into flour. Over time, however, waterwheels were redesigned to help generate electricity to supply power to mills, manufacturing plants, and cities.*

*In this activity, you will build a basic waterwheel and discover how falling water can make it turn.*

**ADULT SUPERVISION REQUIRED**

## You'll Need

⚡ Hot glue gun and glue sticks

⚡ 2 foam board circles, 13-inch (33-centimeter) diameter

⚡ 8 plastic cups, 9 ounces (266 milliliters)

⚡ Scissors

⚡ Wooden dowel, ⁵⁄₁₆-inch (8-millimeter) diameter, or skewer

⚡ Water hose and running water

1. With an adult's help, hot-glue eight plastic cups around the outer edge of a 13-inch (33-centimeter) diameter foam circle as shown. The cups should face the same direction and go all the way around the circle.

2. Glue a second foam circle on top of the cups. Press down to secure. Make sure the cups are glued firmly between both circles, making one solid wheel.

3. Carefully use scissors to poke a hole in the center of each foam circle, then push a wooden dowel rod through both holes. The waterwheel should be able to spin freely around the dowel.

4. Go outside for this step. Hold the dowel rod firmly in your hand with the wheel upright. Hold a water hose above the waterwheel, letting the water flow into the open tops of the plastic cups. What happens?

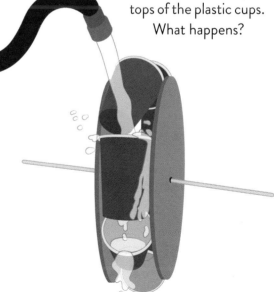

# A Book, Radio Transmission, and a Fire

During the time of the Columbian Exposition and the Niagara Falls hydroelectric power plant project, Tesla had continued his frenzied pace of research and invention. In addition, with the publishing help of T. C. Martin, he wrote his first book in 1893, *The Inventions, Researches, and Writings of Nikola Tesla*. With each public appearance and scientific article written by or about him, Tesla gained more fame.

And as he carried on experimentation with the wireless transmission of energy and his Tesla coil, Tesla discovered another phenomenon quite by accident. A second coil in another part of the room (tuned to the same frequency) sparked when the first one operated in the 500,000 cycles per second range. The spark of the first coil "transmitted radio waves through the air; the other received the waves and converted them back into electricity."

Tesla discussed and demonstrated his radio broadcasting results during his St. Louis lecture on March 1, 1893, and in fact, this is the earliest description of radio transmission and reception ever recorded. So, although Italian inventor Guglielmo Marconi has historically been recognized as the first to demonstrate radio communication in 1895, Tesla had the true bragging rights. Unfortunately, the seeds for the "Radio Wars" and patent disputes between the two inventors were planted about this time, and hard feelings would continue to grow over the next few years.

All through 1894, Tesla developed and continually tested and improved a "small portable radio transmitting station." He could hardly wait until spring when the Hudson River would be ice-free, so he could take a steamship north toward Albany and test how far he could go and still receive transmission signals on his radio—figuring about 50 miles.

Things were going exceptionally well for Tesla at this point. He had more investors to finance his work, including Edward Dean Adams from the Niagara Falls hydroelectric power station project, and one of Tesla's first supporters, Alfred S. Brown. Together with several other men, they formed the Nikola Tesla Company, which would "manufacture and sell machinery, generators, motors, electrical apparatus, etc."

So, with his finances covered, the Current War behind him, the Niagara Falls station in the works, and the anticipation of being the first person to transmit a radio signal over a long distance, Tesla was justifiably satisfied with his life and career. Moreover, his friend and self-appointed publicist T. C. Martin was planning to release yet another article about Tesla's oscillator and inventions in the April 1895 issue of the *Century* magazine. Tesla's fame was at an all-time high, and his star was sure to grow even brighter in the eyes of the world.

Unfortunately, this good fortune did not last. On March 13, 1895, around 2:30 AM, Tesla's laboratory on South Fifth Avenue caught fire. The building was destroyed, and he lost everything—expensive equipment, apparatuses, models, notes, papers, and plans. Nothing was insured, and as one biographer stated, the work of half a lifetime was ruined. It has also been suggested that the blaze might have started "from a gas jet on the first floor near oil-soaked rags" which Tesla had been using during his research of possibly finding a potentially lucrative "means of producing liquid oxygen."

Tesla was devastated and kept to his room for days, which worried his friends. His technological advancements and discoveries were now reduced to setbacks and delays. It would take months, or possibly even years, for him to recover what he'd lost. All research had to be put on hold as he tried to rebuild or replace the basic equipment for a new lab. Ironically, Thomas Edison offered Tesla the use of his West Orange, New Jersey, workshop until different arrangements could be made. As an inventor himself, perhaps Edison understood Tesla's grief over losing everything he'd worked so hard to build. Whatever the reason, Tesla was grateful for a place to work until he was able to move into a new lab on Houston Street in New York City several weeks later.

The fiery interruption in Tesla's career and the temporary delay of his radio transmission work certainly gave Marconi more time to experiment and transmit his own one-mile radio message in Morse code at the end of 1895. By June 1896, he successfully transmitted radio waves several miles with a radio transmission and receiving system and applied for a British patent.

Anyone who knew anything about Tesla's radio transmission work and patents would have

**Nikola Tesla, circa 1896.**
*Tesla Universe*

recognized his ideas and concepts embedded into Marconi's system, but Marconi repeatedly claimed that he knew nothing about his competitor's discoveries. These assertions only created more friction and antagonism between the two men. At this time, Tesla also figured out that the *international* race to be recognized as the first in radio was on the line. He needed to get his new lab in order, start over, and get back to work.

# GUGLIELMO MARCONI

Guglielmo (pronounced goo-YELL-moe) Marconi, an Italian Irish inventor and electrical engineer, was born in Bologna, Italy, on April 25, 1874, to Giuseppe and Annie Jameson Marconi. His father's family was of Italian nobility, and his mother's family had founded the lucrative Jameson Irish Whiskey distillers in Ireland. Guglielmo had an older brother named Alfonso.

The Marconi family was very wealthy, and Annie, especially, loved to travel often with her sons. Because of this, the boys were privately educated for the most part. Guglielmo was intelligent, but he apparently did not do very well with most of his studies.

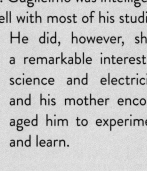

He did, however, show a remarkable interest in science and electricity, and his mother encouraged him to experiment and learn.

**Guglielmo Marconi, circa 1908.** *Library of Congress Prints and Photographs Division, Pach Brothers*

Between 1892 and 1894, Guglielmo attended traditional school in both Florence and at the Livorno Technical Institute, but as he found he would rather spend time doing his own experiments, he left the institute. His father was not happy, but his mother was supportive and encouraging.

He'd read articles by the late Heinrich Hertz, a German physicist who had proven that electromagnetic waves did exist, and he was intrigued by the idea that radio waves could be used to communicate without wires. So, he built a lab at the family's estate and began experimenting with an induction coil, a Morse key, and a sparking gap, along with a simple detector. Within a year, he had sent and received signals from up to two miles away. Marconi took out a patent in 1896, and the British Royal Navy installed some of his equipment on its ships.

In 1901, Marconi transmitted a radio signal across the Atlantic Ocean from Cornwall, England, to Newfoundland, Canada. This feat was important as people had always believed that the radio waves would be lost as the earth curved over that long of a distance. But in fact, Marconi transmitted the signal in Morse code over 2000 miles.

Between 1900 and 1912, Marconi patented several inventions, and in 1909 he shared the Nobel Prize in Physics with Karl Ferdinand Braun for "their contributions to the development of wireless telegraphy." When World War I began in 1914, Marconi

served in the Italian military, moving quickly through the ranks, and was awarded honors of distinction. After the war, he continued researching and inventing and went on to receive many awards, medals, and honorary doctorates from several universities. In 1921 he was even made a marquis, a rank of nobility just below a duke, by King Victor Emanuel III of Italy.

Marconi was married twice. He had three daughters and a son with his first wife, and one daughter with his second wife. Guglielmo Marconi died on July 20, 1937, in Rome, Italy, from a heart attack at age 63.

# Of Radios and Robots

In the late 1890s, Tesla regularly gave lectures describing his work in several New York cities, but he also received a special accolade from his native land at the end of 1896. He was made an honorary member of the Yugoslav Academy of Sciences and Arts in Zagreb. In fact, Tesla was considered almost a divine being to people of the Balkans, and in years to come, both Serbs and Croats would argue over who had the most claim to Tesla's heritage.

Tesla also continued to experiment with transmitting radio signals over long distances, and on September 2, 1897, he filed two basic patents on equipment that could generate, transmit, and receive radio signals. The patents (numbers 645,576 and 649,621) weren't granted until March 1900, but they were already in place when Marconi applied to file an American patent on his wireless system on November 10, 1900. Marconi's application was turned down because his ideas were too similar to Tesla's, but Marconi kept revising and resubmitting his applications unsuccessfully. This did not keep him from trying to win public support and attention for his system, however, and he even garnered endorsements from Thomas Edison and other respected scientists and inventors. Unsurprisingly, the "Radio War" would continue to rage.

Tesla's work in the late 1890s was not limited to radio. Indeed, he was investigating many other fascinating subjects at the same time. One such interest was developing remote-controlled devices,

**Tesla's teleautomaton, a radio-controlled boat.** *Tesla Universe*

which he called teleautomatons—or wireless robots, an idea he claimed he'd thought of years earlier. Of course, the laboratory fire had delayed his research, but he filed patent number 613,809 on July 1, 1898. His application listed the patent name as "Method of and Apparatus for Controlling Mechanism of Moving Vessels or Vehicles," and it was granted on November 8 of that year.

In many ways, the timing of Tesla's patent application was remarkable. On February 15, 1898, a mysterious explosion had sunk the USS *Maine*, an American dreadnaught ship on a "mission of friendly courtesy," which was docked in the harbor at Havana, Cuba. Of the 350 sailors on board, 266 were killed, and US citizens were outraged. Since Cuba was battling for independence from Spain, Americans cast suspicious eyes toward Spain and blamed that country for the destruction. With a cry of "Remember the Maine!" the United States formally declared war on Spain on April 25, 1898.

Under the circumstances, any technology that might be weaponized for military uses was of the utmost interest to the American public. But Tesla amazed and perhaps baffled audiences when he demonstrated the world's first remote-controlled vessel at the first Electrical Exhibition at Madison Square Garden on December 8, 1898. He refused to let newspaper reporters see his wireless teleautomaton boat demonstration, because he thought they'd make fun of his far-fetched ideas. But the spectators who did attend didn't quite know what to make of the "small, odd-looking wooden-hulled boat scooting around in a pond especially built for it in the great auditorium."

Tesla didn't disclose all the special features of his vessel to attendees, as he hoped the navy might seriously consider buying and using his design. If that happened, he knew the navy would insist upon secrecy. But he did claim that his device "could attack and destroy a whole armada—destroy it utterly in an hour, and the enemy never have a sight of their antagonists or know what power destroyed them."

Unfortunately, US War Department officials thought Tesla's idea was impractical and impossible. Many called it a "wild fancy." His teleautomaton was actually a forerunner to today's guided weapons and vehicles, but it was far too advanced for the times. Not until 1918 was such technology developed and used by the military, consequently after Tesla's patents had already expired.

By the time Tesla took part in the exhibition at Madison Square Garden, he'd had years of positive publicity. But by not allowing reporters to see his teleautomaton in action, he might've made a mistake. Other participating inventors, including Marconi and Edison, were more willing for their inventions or designs to be publicized, and therefore they received more praise in the media—while Tesla was criticized by many for his secretiveness and wild ideas. Even T. C. Martin wrote an unfavorable editorial about him in *Electrical Engineer*, which hurt Tesla deeply and eventually led to the end of their long friendship.

And of course, Tesla was disappointed that the navy declined to buy his design, as he truly believed his boat could bring an end to war and save lives. But another reason was that he was

# MAKE A SODA BOTTLE SUBMARINE

*Nikola Tesla's remote-controlled teleautomaton was a sensation, but it was far ahead of its time. Tesla always believed that his submarine torpedo boat would have been a great naval weapon. In this activity, you will make a soda bottle submarine.*

---

**ADULT SUPERVISION REQUIRED**

## You'll Need

⚡ 20-ounce (591-milliliter) plastic soda bottle
⚡ Hammer and nail
⚡ Scissors
⚡ 10 pennies
⚡ Waterproof tape, such as duct tape
⚡ Bendable plastic straw (or plastic tubing)
⚡ Modeling clay or putty
⚡ Large basin (optional)

1. With an adult's help, make a hole in the center of a plastic bottle cap using a hammer and nail. The opening should be large enough for a straw (or plastic tubing) to fit through.

2. Use scissors to punch three holes down the side of a plastic bottle, as shown in the illustration.

3. Make two stacks of five pennies. Wrap each group in tape so the stacks stay together.

4. Tape one group of coins near the top of the bottle and the other group near the bottom, in line with the holes you punched. Make sure you don't cover up the holes. This is the bottom of the submarine.

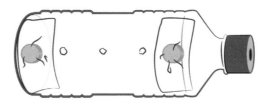

5. Place the flexible end of a drinking straw through the hole in the bottle cap, with the bendy part of the straw still outside the cap. Use modeling clay or putty to seal the opening around the straw. (If using plastic tubing, putty around the tubing to seal.)

6. Fill a large basin (or a sink) with water and place the submarine on the water surface. It should start to sink as the holes let water into the bottle. If you suck air from the straw, the submarine will sink even faster.

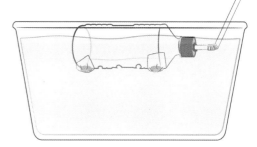

7. Now blow air back into the bottle through the straw. What happens?

As you suck air *out* of the bottle, there is more room for water to flow in, and the submarine sinks. As you blow air back *into* the bottle, the water is forced out. The added air makes the submarine rise.

once again in a financial bind. He never focused on money, as he placed more value on his inventions and invested all he had into research. But expenses incurred during his radio and robot experiments had completely depleted his bank account, and he had nothing left to work with or live on. It was time to find a new investor for his next venture.

## Creating Lightning in Colorado Springs

Tesla had already approached two previous investors, Edward Dean Adams and George Westinghouse, to see if either of them would financially support his continuing research and creation of a cheap (or free) worldwide wireless power distribution system. But neither man was interested in contributing more money. So Tesla spread his net a bit further, hoping to land a wealthy investor who also had an interest in invention or science. His strategy? Go to dinner.

Tesla liked to dine in fine restaurants, and he was a valued guest at places such as Delmonico's and the Waldorf-Astoria's gorgeous dining room. Therefore, the owner of the Waldorf-Astoria, John Jacob Astor IV, was already familiar with the celebrated inventor and considered him a friend. Moreover, as a member of the advisory committee of the Niagara Falls project, he'd worked with Tesla and followed his work with interest. Astor was an inventor himself, and he was also well-known for having served with Teddy Roosevelt and the Rough Riders during the Spanish-American War. And most importantly, he was the heir to a $100 million fortune.

When Astor heard that Tesla desperately needed funds to continue his research, he promised to invest $100,000, with an initial payment of $30,000. In return, he would receive 500 shares in the Nikola Tesla Company, which would give him majority control, and he would also be made director of the company.

There was just one glitch: Astor wanted Tesla to work on perfecting a fluorescent lighting system. But Tesla wanted to devote his time to researching the wireless transmission of power instead. He agreed to honor his patron's wishes—at least until Astor left on an extended trip to Europe right after they completed their business arrangement. Tesla's thoughts? There'd be time later to work on fluorescent lamps.

That settled, Tesla asked trusted colleagues for advice and looked around the country for a site to build a secret experimental transmission station to try out his latest ideas. He needed a lot of room because his coils were "producing 4,000,000 volts—sparks jumping from walls to ceilings [were] a fire hazard." His Westinghouse patent attorney, Leonard E. Curtis, sent word that he knew of just the place: Colorado Springs. Curtis was associated with the Colorado Springs Electric Company, and he reported that he'd worked it out for Tesla to have both free electricity and land on which to build a new lab. He'd even arranged accommodations at the Alta Vista Hotel.

Tesla was overjoyed and started making plans. He shipped machinery to Colorado in the early part of 1899 and arrived there himself on May 18. He immediately hired a carpenter to start building

**John Jacob Astor IV, circa 1909.** *George Grantham Bain Collection, Prints and Photographs Division, Library of Congress, LC-USZ62-40303*

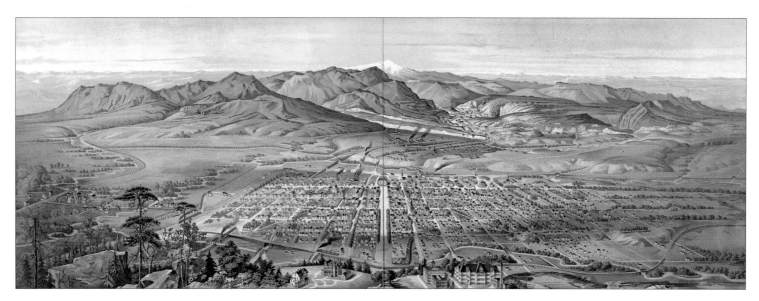

(left) **Colorado Springs with Pikes Peak in the background in the late 1890s.** *Tesla Universe*

(below) **Exterior view of Tesla's Colorado Springs lab with ball lowered, 1899.** *Tesla Universe*

his lab, which looked like a big barn with a center section of the roof that could be opened and closed. Tesla also "devised a telescoping mast that could hoist a thirty-inch copper covered ball to a height of 142 feet. To stabilize the mast, [he] added a twenty-five-foot tower to the roof of the station."

During the late 1800s, Colorado Springs was still very rural, although it was already becoming a popular tourist destination, as Pikes Peak was close by. But overall, the high altitude and mountainous terrain were just right for Tesla's experimental needs, and his lab was located about one mile east of town.

As another plus, Colorado Springs was known for dramatic lightning storms, which Tesla planned to observe and study. He was always fascinated and awed by any form of energy, but especially by these flashing and crackling bursts of power in the sky that generated several hundred million volts of electricity per flash. Yet, little did the locals

realize that Tesla had plans to create lighting of his own using the most gigantic Tesla coil he'd ever built. However, the tall fence around the property and the attached KEEP OUT—GREAT DANGER sign might possibly have tipped them off.

A double exposure photo of Tesla sitting beside his oscillator, or magnifying transmitter, one of the largest Tesla coils ever built. This famous 1899 photo was a publicity stunt, and Tesla was not actually sitting beside the coil as it was sparking.

*Tesla Universe*

Tesla thought he could transmit light, information, and power vast distances without using any wires, but he needed "to be free of the disturbing influences in the city which [made] it very difficult to tune circuits." He believed that the earth was electrically charged, and that energy could be transmitted easily and cheaply through the upper atmosphere above the planet—or possibly through the earth itself. Either way, no wires would be needed.

Tesla's previous inventions already included the necessary equipment to generate high frequencies and voltages, and of course, he'd perfected the Tesla coil, which produced four million volts. But to "power a device capable of making transmissions on a global scale," he'd need an even bigger and more powerful coil. His solution? A "magnifying transmitter," which was just a monster-sized Tesla coil.

Under his supervision, Tesla's two assistants created this huge Tesla coil, or magnifying transmitter (also called an oscillator), and placed it on the lab floor right below the retractable part of the roof. Then they attached the telescoping pole topped with the large copper ball, which could be raised above the building, to the top of the oscillator. Tesla described his apparatus as a "resonant transformer" and said it was possible for it to generate 100 million volts. And later he would claim that this magnifying transmitter was his greatest invention.

Although Tesla was not normally a notetaker, he did record his experiment results, theories, observations, and mathematical equations during his stay in Colorado. He also made photographs of some of his experiments. He no longer trusted his memory to retain such valuable information, and he didn't want to lose even the smallest detail. In fact, the value he put on his work during this time is evident, as his Colorado Springs notebook was discovered among his possessions many years after his death.

Tesla used AC power from the El Paso Electrical Station, a few miles away, to service his lab, and he was able to step up the voltage as needed. And as he was experimenting with the magnifying transmitter, he discovered that it could

# EXPLORE EARTH'S MAGNETIC FIELD

*The earth is like a giant magnet that produces its own magnetic field. Nikola Tesla believed he could generate power from this magnetic field, and many of his experiments and inventions were based on this assumption.*

*Of course, the earth has a north pole and a south pole, but its magnetic poles are not in the same place as its true poles. When you use a compass, the needle will always point to earth's magnetic pole. In this activity, you will use a compass to follow the path of the magnetic field from one pole on a magnet to the other. You will also learn how to make your own compass with a needle and magnet.*

## You'll Need

⚡ Bar magnet

⚡ Compass

⚡ Steel needle

⚡ Bowl of water

⚡ 2-inch (5-centimeter) diameter circle cut from paper

1. Place a bar magnet on a flat surface and move a compass toward the magnet's south pole. What happens?

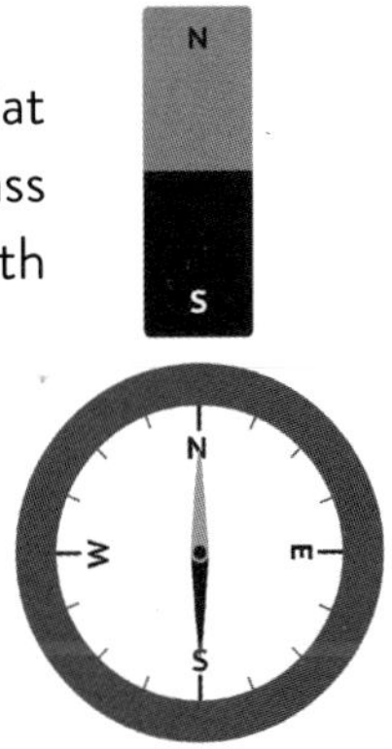

2. Next, move the compass slowly toward the magnet's north pole. What happens to the needle? (The needle on the compass will always follow the line of force of the magnetic field of the bar magnet. Therefore, the compass needle will always point *away from* the south pole.)

3. Now it's time to make your own compass. First, stroke the magnet down the full length of the needle, from the eye to the point. Do this about 40 to 50 times, always stroking in the same direction. This process causes iron atoms in the needle to line up in the same direction, and the needle will become magnetized.

4. Thread the magnetized needle through the paper circle as shown, then lay the circle on the surface of a bowl of water. Both ends of the needle should be above the water line.

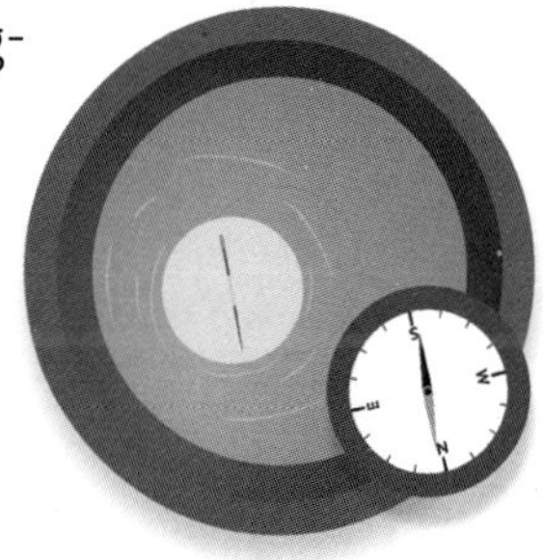

5. Observe what happens. (The circle should rotate but finally stop with the magnetized needle pointing north.)

6. Check the direction of the floating needle with your compass. The new magnetic field of the needle should have lined up with the earth's magnetic field.

produce "lighting" as powerful as the bolts that naturally flashed across the sky during a storm. In fact, the ground became electrified for miles around, and the noise it created rivaled the boom of cannons. And although Tesla and his assistants wore special cork-bottomed shoes to be safe, it was reported that pedestrians some distances away saw sparks between their shoes and the ground as they walked. Even horses grazing a half mile away from the lab received a shock through their metal shoes and galloped away wildly. Unsurprisingly, fires in the lab were also common.

The people of Colorado Springs were obviously unaware of what the foreign inventor was doing in his top-secret lab out on the prairie, but on one midsummer night they were really left in the dark—literally. Raising the pole and copper ball through the lab's roof, Tesla told his assistant to turn on the equipment's power at his signal. He positioned himself where he could see through the open roof, shouted for the assistant to pull the switch, and then watched with ecstasy as bright blue bolts of lightning, over 100 feet long, shot out from the copper ball on top of the pole. The ground shook, and the noise was thunderous. It was a spectacular display! Then—nothing. The lab was plunged into darkness and it became eerily silent.

At first, Tesla believed the electric company had shut him down by cutting off his power, and he was furious. But he soon found out that he had overloaded and blown out the company's dynamo and set it on fire. The whole area had lost power, and neither the town's citizens nor the power company officials were happy with the inventor. Within a week, the power was restored, but predictably, Tesla was informed that he'd no longer be receiving free power for his lab.

**The front view of Tesla's Colorado Springs lab with the ball raised in 1899.**
*Tesla Universe*

## The Mars Mystery

Another peculiar thing happened to Tesla before he returned to New York. Late one night while working with his powerful radio receiver, he received three short radio signals. Although he was unsure at first where they came from, Tesla eventually concluded it was communication from outer space—from Mars. Initially, he was reluctant to share his discovery, as he could "anticipate the ridicule of his fellow scientists when they heard the news." But in the end, he was too excited not to share his "Martian theory" in several published articles.

At the time, many Americans were obsessed with the idea of Martians or life on other planets, so Tesla's revelation caused two reactions from the public—excitement over such a possibility or the notion that crazy, delusional Tesla had finally gone off the deep end. Of course, the media was ruthless, and many reporters and scientists made fun of him, just as he'd expected.

Today, scientists believe that Tesla's equipment probably did receive signals from space, although not from Mars. According to biographer Lisa J. Aldrich, it was probably "from the stars via electromagnetic radiation. The universe emits wavelengths of energy which we call static when we hear it between radio stations on the dial. Tesla may have been the first person to receive and listen to radio waves from outer space."

For Tesla, his supposed discovery of communication with Mars was just a bonus to what he was trying to do on his own planet, which was to create a wireless power system. He once said, "The same principle may be employed with good effects for the transmission of news to all parts of the Earth. . . . Every city on the globe could be on an immense circuit. . . . A message sent from New York would be in England, Africa, and Australia in an instant. What a grand thing that would be." It was almost as if he could see into the future, proving once again that he was a man ahead of his time.

By late 1899, Tesla had finished his work in Colorado and was satisfied with his results. The dawn of a new century slipped by as he dismantled his lab and prepared to leave. He was back in New York City by mid-January 1900, and he immediately began filing new patents for the work he'd completed out west.

## Money from Morgan

Tesla also began making big plans to build a world radio center, but he'd already spent all the money he'd received from John Jacob Astor IV on his Colorado Springs experimental transmission station and investigations. Astor didn't offer any more financial assistance to the broke inventor for his new project, as he was probably upset with Tesla for running off to Colorado instead of following through on his promise to work on the fluorescent lighting system. In any case, Tesla now needed a new backer, and he knew just the man: John Pierpont Morgan Sr.

J. P. Morgan, of course, knew about Tesla and his previous financiers and projects. He also recognized that, other than his AC deal with Westinghouse, none of Tesla's inventions had made a profit. Nevertheless, after reading Tesla's newest article in the *Century* magazine about the future of electricity and the possibility of transmitting

## JOHN PIERPONT (J. P.) MORGAN SR.

J. P. Morgan (1837–1913) was one of the wealthiest and most influential men in the world during the late 19th and early 20th centuries. He was a well-known banker, Wall Street tycoon, industrialist, and, most important to Tesla, a capitalist who invested financially in promising business ventures—and inventors.

Morgan, however, did not hesitate to pull his money from failing projects, nor did he shy away from corporate takeovers and mergers. He was a key player in the merger and formation of new corporations, including General Electric, US Steel, International Harvester, and AT&T, and he was a leading figure in the country's new Progressive Era. Although many people didn't agree with his tactics or what they considered to be his meddling with America's economy, he helped modernize and transform American business as no other man of his time.

**J. P. Morgan Sr. in 1902.** *Library of Congress Prints and Photographs Division, Photoprint by Pach Brothers, LC-USZ61-327*

information and messages wirelessly around the world, he became more intrigued. It would be a huge advantage for a savvy investor, such as himself, to have the ability to communicate instantly with stock exchanges and banks around the world. Moreover, Tesla assured Morgan that his investment would soon be worth millions.

## Wardenclyffe

Skeptical or not, Morgan agreed to loan Tesla $150,000 (the inventor used his radio patents as collateral) to build a transmission tower and power plant, although they both knew it would take much more money than that to complete the project. Regardless, Tesla found and purchased 200 acres in an isolated farming area near Shoreham, Long Island, thanks to his contact, James D. Warden of the Suffolk Land Company. The property was also near a railroad, which was important for bringing in builders and supplies. Tesla named the site Wardenclyffe, after James Warden, as well as the nearby cliffs overlooking the Long Island Sound.

Once again, Tesla's goals were not completely in sync with his investor's plans. Both he and Morgan wanted a tower built to transmit wireless communication worldwide, but Tesla also had a bigger goal in mind, which he kept to himself, as Morgan probably would've refused to invest in the project. Tesla wanted to build a 187-foot tower with a shaft sunk 120 feet into the ground and top it with a 57-ton steel dome to transmit wireless electrical energy around the globe. There was a significant difference between the two intentions, but Tesla stayed quiet and proceeded with the construction plans for the Wardenclyffe tower, plant, and laboratory in 1901. He hired his renowned architect friend, Stanford White, to design the laboratory. At first, Tesla traveled from Manhattan to the site and back each day by train, but eventually he rented a cottage near the property for a year to supervise the work.

## Marconi's Coup and Morgan's Refusal

The rising Wardenclyffe tower could be seen by Connecticut residents across the Sound, and what a magnificent structure it was! The building crew continued to make progress, and by November 1901, steam boilers and engines were being installed in the powerhouse. That brick building was situated some distance away from the tower, to protect workers from stray "lightning bolts" that might be emitted from the domed antenna. Despite the continuous need for more money, everything seemed to be going well. But Tesla's grand plans were about to take a downward spiral. Again.

On December 12, 1901, Tesla, along with everyone else in the world, got the news that Guglielmo Marconi had successfully transmitted the letter *S* from Cornwall, England, to Newfoundland, Canada—more than 2,000 miles across the Atlantic Ocean. He'd beaten Tesla to the draw, although very few realized that Marconi had used at least 17 of Tesla's patents in the process. Marconi was proclaimed "father" of radio, while Tesla was deprived of the credit he deserved.

Eventually, J. P. Morgan began to question Tesla's plans. If Marconi could wirelessly transmit

(left) **Tesla's lab and uncompleted Wardenclyffe tower in 1902.** *Tesla Universe*

(below) **An illustration depicting Tesla's vision of how Wardenclyffe tower would work in full operation. His "world wireless system" tower was to have looked quite different when finished.** *Tesla Universe*

# MAKE A WAVE

*Waves are all around us! Sound, light, radio—all travel in waves. Even the ocean waves crashing onto the shore follow the same pattern of movement. If a wave hits something solid that it can't pass through, it will bounce back, or reflect, in the opposite direction.*

*Nikola Tesla worked with what he called non-Hertzian waves throughout much of his career. In fact, he planned to transmit wireless power around the globe from Wardenclyffe. Tesla always insisted that his electrical transmissions were longitudinal (running lengthwise instead of across) in nature, making them similar to sound waves.*

*In this activity, you will be able to see how radio waves (and in fact, all kinds of waves) move.*

## You'll Need

⚡ 30 wooden skewers

⚡ 60 gum drops

⚡ Two sturdy wooden kitchen chairs

⚡ Duct tape

1. Push a single gum drop on each end of 30 wooden skewers.

2. Set two chairs about 6 to 7 feet (2 meters) apart, back to back. Stretch a piece of duct tape between the chairs and attach the tape to the chairbacks, making sure the sticky side is turned up.

3. Center and press the skewers along the sticky side of the tape, leaving about 1½ to 2 inches (4 to 5 centimeters) between skewers. Leave about 12 inches (30 centimeters) of the tape empty on both ends.

4. Press another length of duct tape (sticky side down) onto the skewers to hold them in place.

5. Tap one end of the "wave" to see how it moves from one end to the other. It should "bounce back" when it reaches the far chair.

You've just witnessed the reflection of a wave. Pretty sweet, right?

communication without building an expensive facility, why was Wardenclyffe even necessary? He started to doubt the investment, so Tesla finally told him about his idea of not just sending radio signals from the tower but also transmitting wireless power around the globe.

Because such an achievement would endanger or cheapen his other electric power investments, Morgan refused to provide more money for Wardenclyffe. He also viewed Tesla's change of plans as a breach of contract, and by 1903 he'd withdrawn all support.

Perhaps it was coincidence, or merely one of Tesla's work sessions, but on the night Morgan's last letter arrived declining to send more money, a grand display of "lightning fireworks" was seen coming from the Wardenclyffe tower. According to biographer Margaret Cheney, "Residents watched in awe as blinding streaks shot off the spherical dome, at times lighting up the sky within a radius of hundreds of miles. Take that, Pierpont Morgan, they seemed to say."

OSCILLATION TRANSFORMER

INDUCTION MOTOR

WORLD WIRELESS TELEPHONE TRANSMITTER

TELAUTOMATON

STEAM & GAS TURBINE

NIKOLA TESLA COMPANY

8 West 40th St.
TEL. 9090 BRYANT
New York

*Nikola Tesla*

# 5

# TRIALS, SUCCESSES, AND SADNESS

*The world was not prepared for it. It was too far ahead of time.*
—Nikola Tesla, on his magnifying transmitter

After J. P. Morgan backed out of the Wardenclyffe project, Nikola Tesla sought other investors, but he had very little success. When other capitalists heard that the shrewd financier Morgan wanted no further part of such a venture, they too were wary. And what money Tesla did manage to raise only went to pay off some of the debts he'd already incurred during construction. His military friend, Lieutenant Richmond P. Hobson, stepped in and tried again to interest the navy in Tesla's robotic inventions,

**Nikola Tesla Company logo and Tesla's signature.** *Tesla Universe*

hoping that would bring some financial stability to the inventor's life. Once more, the navy declined.

Tesla was running out of ideas, money, and wealthy investors, but he did file several patents pertaining to his Wardenclyffe experiments in 1902, although they weren't granted until 1914. In addition, some doctors and other health professionals had an interest in a small Tesla coil, called a therapeutic oscillator, that was manufactured at Wardenclyffe. The coil was used in medical equipment that treated arthritis and other joint diseases, and fortunately for Tesla, this side business earned a small profit. So, with the little bit of money he scraped together, he tried his best to stay afloat and continued to work through 1903 and 1904. But creditors were continuously hounding him for repayment on equipment, supplies, and building materials, and workers obviously wanted to be paid.

Next, he discovered that the power company in Colorado Springs was suing for the costs of the electricity he'd used at his experimental lab while working there in 1899. Since Leonard Curtis had assured him that his power was to have been free (at least before the generator fire catastrophe), it's possible that Tesla might've been blindsided by this lawsuit. Regardless, the Colorado Springs experimental station was torn down, and the lumber was sold to pay the $180 judgment against him.

Later in 1904, things got even worse. Tesla found out that US Patent Office had reversed its previous decision and given Guglielmo Marconi the patent for the invention of the radio. Perhaps it was just a coincidence, but this decision was made right after Thomas Edison and J. P. Morgan became investors in Marconi's company, which would later become the Radio Corporation of America (RCA). Whatever the reason for the surprising patent decision reversal, Tesla was upset.

In 1915, Tesla finally filed a lawsuit against Marconi himself, stating that the Italian inventor had infringed upon patent rights that had previously been awarded to him (Tesla). Unfortunately, Tesla did not have much money to fight costly court battles against a large corporation. Not until after his death in 1943 did the US Supreme Court finally rule that Tesla, and not Marconi, was the true inventor of the radio.

## Winding Down Wardenclyffe

By 1905, his financial troubles were unmanageable, and Tesla finally had to give up his dream of building a wireless power transmission center and close the Wardenclyffe station. The equipment was taken away to satisfy debts, and the workers left to find other jobs. Tesla had even put two mortgages on the property worth $20,000 with the Waldorf-Astoria's manager, George C. Boldt, to cover his hotel bills and luxurious lifestyle during this time. Ten years later, when he could not afford to pay the hotel anything at all, he would have to sign over the Wardenclyffe deed itself to the Waldorf-Astoria. In Tesla's own words to one of his assistants, "Troubles and troubles, but they do just seem to track me." And indeed, they did.

After the failed Wardenclyffe project, Tesla became dangerously ill and suffered another mental collapse. It seems that overwork and intense, constant brain activity contributed to his pattern of depression and mental breakdowns through the years, but the discouragement of being unable to finish his world power station played a part too. And although he did recover and develop other technology and inventions after the Wardenclyffe period, he never again attempted such a large or ambitious project.

## Inventing Again

In 1906, Tesla realized that many of his peers, and much of the press, now believed he was a crazy dreamer, rather than a practical inventor. In truth, they often doubted his abilities and his sanity. He'd lost a great deal of credibility, so he knew it was important that he come up with a new (and commercially successful) invention straightaway. Perhaps he thought of the waterwheel he'd built while he was still a little boy and found inspiration—he decided he would invent a new kind of turbine.

A normal turbine is a rotary mechanical device that uses the flow of liquids, steam, or gas pushing against its blades or paddles to make it revolve quickly and create energy. Such machines were used to generate electricity from the falling waters at the Niagara Falls hydroelectric power plant. But Tesla purposed to create a turbine that had no blades or propellers at all. He knew that the thickness (viscosity) of whatever medium flowed against the blades determined the level of resistance, and that any friction could slow down the speed of the turbine.

Tesla's goal was to replace the turbine's blades with a row of discs stacked together with only small spaces between each disc. These discs would be attached to a central shaft inside a sealed metal holder. When fluid passed the discs, they would turn the shaft, which could be used to create electricity. This method of using a spiral path for the discs would increase the speed of the turbine. And Tesla's new lower resistance design also meant that almost any amount of power could be obtained from it using a much smaller engine. In fact, the first model weighed less than 10 pounds and developed 30 horsepower. He later built much larger ones that developed 200 horsepower.

Tesla predicted limitless uses for his new turbine and thought it could be manufactured far less expensively than traditional designs. Gasoline, steam, water, or wind could fuel the turbine, and this meant it had the potential to power cars, planes, ocean liners, trains, and other modes of transportation. It could also be used in the areas of hydraulics, refrigeration, agriculture, mining, irrigation, and other industries.

Tesla went public with his idea on his 50th birthday, July 10, 1906, by writing an article describing his newest invention. The concept of a bladeless turbine caused a stir, and he received praise from other inventors and people all over the world. He initially hoped to patent the design, then sell the patent to an interested manufacturing company. He desperately longed for his money woes to be resolved, but in the end, he was destined to be disappointed.

An 18-inch Tesla turbine with cover removed to display the rotor. *Tesla Universe*

Although his concept for the bladeless turbine did win acclaim, it was simply another idea too far ahead of its time. Tesla ran into problems trying to refine his model, and he had trouble finding appropriate materials to work with. He would receive the patent for the bladeless turbine in 1913, but the device wouldn't be perfected and put into commercial use until many years later.

## Flivver Planes

In May 1907, Tesla was inducted into the New York Academy of Sciences, a welcome honor amid his many problems. And that same year, he opened an office at 165 Broadway. At the time, he was still hoping for fortunes from his bladeless turbine design, and he took the chance that he'd be able to pay for the new space. Moreover, since he no longer had his Wardenclyffe lab, he needed a permanent area where he could work on innovative ideas and meet with prospective clients or corporate officials who might want to hire him as an electrical engineering consultant. In truth, he was also still hoping to find additional backers who were willing to revive the Wardenclyffe project, although that never happened.

One of Tesla's innovations that consumed his time and effort over the next few years was a flying machine, which he called a flivver plane. Of course, the Wright brothers had made their famous first flight at Kitty Hawk, North Carolina, in 1903, and Americans were obsessed with the concept of air travel. Tesla, too, believed that it was just a matter of time until air machines replaced sailing vessels as the main mode of travel.

But he wanted to create a flying machine that incorporated his bladeless turbine design and could be powered by wirelessly transmitted electricity from stations on the ground. It would also be able to take off and land vertically and fly both horizontally and vertically. (This is also called a VTOL [vertical takeoff and landing] aircraft.) His flivver plane design had the characteristics of both an airplane and a helicopter, but it couldn't technically be classified as either.

In his own words, from the October 15, 1911, article in the *New York Herald*, Tesla explained, "My flying machine will have neither wings nor propellers. You might see it on the ground and you would never guess that it was a flying machine. Yet it will be able to move at will through the air in any direction with perfect safety, higher speeds than have yet been reached, regardless of weather . . . or downward currents. It can remain absolutely stationary in the air, even in a wind, for great length of time."

Tesla did file for patents on his flivver plane, but they were not granted until 1928, when he was 72 years old. Many years later, a similar aircraft was built by the military, but Tesla never made a prototype of the flivver plane himself. The concept was amazing, but the untimeliness of his idea and the prohibitive cost to develop a model probably kept him from following through.

Other plans found after his death, such as designs for flying cars and spaceships, probably seemed like things from science fiction novels to most people. It's fun to imagine what Tesla would say if he could see the many modern inventions (including some of his own) that people of his day would've deemed impossible. And who knows what the future still holds!

## Marconi—Again!

In 1909, it was announced that Guglielmo Marconi and Ferdinand Braun would share the Nobel Prize in Physics for "their contributions to the development of wireless telegraphy." What a bitter pill for Tesla to swallow! Obviously, he felt that he'd been cheated out of his rightful recognition, and he resented the fact that Marconi was still being praised for inventing the radio—after using 17 of *his* patents. Tesla still couldn't bring a lawsuit against Marconi—he simply lacked the funds to do so—but he did not forget about it. The Radio War had been raging between the two inventors for almost two decades, and it would continue for many more years until justice prevailed.

## Tears for Twain

Mark Twain (Samuel Clemens) had been an important figure in Tesla's life ever since he'd read the author's earliest works as a boy on his sickbed back in Gospić. When Twain died of a heart attack on April 21, 1910, Tesla was distressed and grieved deeply. The two men had become fast friends when Tesla moved to the United States, and Twain had been a regular visitor to the Tesla lab, sometimes

even participating in experiments. He'd also been one of Tesla's biggest supporters and encouragers during his darkest days.

Twain's death was just one of the many factors that seemed to affect Tesla's spirit in the early 1910s, and friends noticed that his behavior, while always a bit eccentric, became even stranger. Another sad event occurred when John Jacob Astor IV, who'd taken a chance on investing in Tesla's work in 1899, perished when the ill-fated RMS *Titanic* hit an iceberg and sank in the North Atlantic Ocean in April 1912. It's true that Astor had been upset with Tesla over the Colorado Springs incident, but the two had since reconciled, and Astor's tragic death was a blow.

**Mark Twain and Nikola Tesla in 1894.** *Tesla Universe*

# DESIGN A FLYING MACHINE

*Nikola Tesla was always fascinated by flying machines, even when he was a boy. In fact, when he landed in America, he carried a drawing for a flying machine in his pocket. Although Tesla envisioned, designed, and filed a patent request on what he called a flivver plane in 1911, he did not receive the patent until 1928. Tesla's flying machine would be considered a VTOL (vertical takeoff and landing) apparatus today. Experiment with various "flying machine" designs!*

## You'll Need

⚡ 1 sheet multipurpose 24-pound copy paper, 8½ x 11 inches (216 x 279 millimeters), plus extras for modifications

⚡ Small paper clips

1. Fold a sheet of stiff paper in half vertically, then fold each top corner down to the center fold.

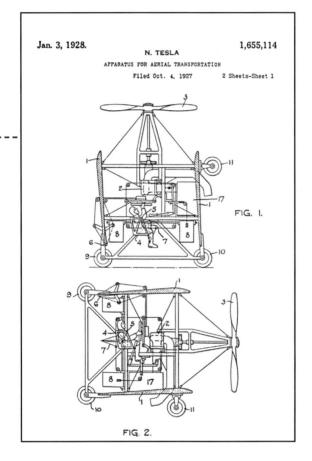

**Nikola Tesla's drawing for his "Apparatus for Aerial Transportation." He patented the design in 1924.**
*United States Patent and Trademark Office*

2. Fold the top of the paper down so it touches 1 inch (3 centimeters) from the bottom. (It will look like an envelope.)

3. Fold both of the "new" top corners to the center line. There will be a small triangular flap in the center—fold it up.

4. Fold the plane in half at the center line. The triangular flap should show on the outside.

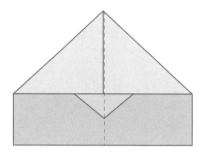

5. Fold down wings on both sides. If you want, you can fold the wings more than once, like an accordion.

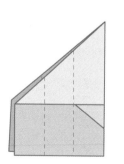

6. Add weight to the wings or nose of the plane with small paper clips. This is your "starter" plane. Toss the plane a few times to see how it flies.

7. Now modify the design. Try the paper clips at different locations or change the folds on the wings. Experiment with each modification until you discover the best design!

Even J. P. Morgan's death in 1913 seemed to affect Tesla. The two could hardly be called friends, but Morgan's life and activities had often overlapped and influenced Tesla's in many ways. Tesla was always a highly sensitive person, and these changes probably unsettled him. Perhaps this was why he started picking up and caring for wounded pigeons in his hotel room—a compassionate habit that would become more bizarre as he grew older.

# THE *TITANIC* AND THE WIRELESS RADIO SYSTEM

The RMS *Titanic* was a British White Star Line ocean liner. It left Southampton, England, on April 10, 1912, on its maiden voyage bound for New York City. At the time, the *Titanic* was the largest passenger ship in the world and deemed "unsinkable."

Guglielmo Marconi had been invited to sail on the *Titanic* free of charge, as his wireless radio system, which was named for him, had been installed in the ship's radio room. He chose to sail to the United States two days earlier on the RMS *Lusitania*. His wife and children were to follow on the *Titanic*, but one of the children became sick and they were unable to sail.

The radio system wasn't perfect, but Marconi operators could communicate with other ships and operators on land by using Morse code. The ship's purser would bring messages to the radio operators that passengers wanted to send to someone on shore, and it was the operators' job to forward these "Marconigrams" to the recipients via the radiotelegraph transmitter.

In the early hours of April 15, 1912, the *Titanic* collided with a massive iceberg in the North Atlantic Ocean and began to sink. Pandemonium set in. Half-filled lifeboats were lowered into the water, stranding many passengers still on board. The operators immediately began sending out frantic SOS signals over the wireless transmitter, hoping nearby vessels would hear the distress signals and come help.

The SS *Californian* was only about five miles away but did not respond. The *Californian*'s radio operator had turned off the wireless and gone to bed only minutes before the *Titanic* struck the iceberg. Although people on board the *Californian* saw flares in the distance, they testified that they didn't realize anything was wrong. However, the radio operator on the RMS *Carpathia*, which was 58 miles away, did hear the SOS. The ship raced toward the *Titanic*, arriving around 4:00 AM. Only 706 people of the 2,028 on board were rescued and carried to New York City aboard the *Carpathia*.

Marconi's wireless system enabled the Marconi operators to call for help, saving many lives. Guglielmo Marconi was hailed a hero.

# COMMUNICATE WITH MORSE CODE

*Morse code was created by Samuel Morse, who invented the telegraph and the system of sending messages by electrical impulses along a wire during the 1830s and 1840s. Using this method, both long and short signals could be sent along the wires, then translated into letters of the alphabet, so messages could be read on the other end.*

*How well can you tap out or read a message in Morse code? Find out!*

1. Using the Morse code chart on this page, decode the following sentence. There is a slash (/) between each word in the sentence.

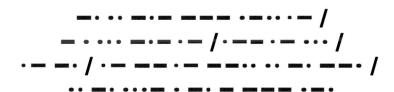

2. Now look at the chart with a friend. Create a message using the dots and dashes to represent letters.

3. Tap it out and see if your friend can decode the message. Then, take turns creating and decoding secret messages.

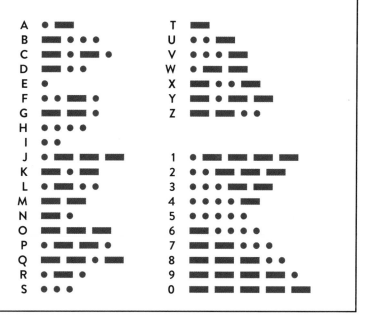

**MORSE CODE CHART**

1. A dash is equal to three dots.
2. The space between parts of the same letter is equal to one dot.
3. The space between two letters is equal to three dots.
4. The space between two words is equal to seven dots.

Answer: Nikola Tesla was an amazing inventor

# THROUGH THE YEARS: 1914–1931

----

*Be alone, that is the secret of invention; be alone, that is when ideas are born.*
—**Nikola Tesla**

----

The year 1914 began with another death that greatly affected Nikola Tesla. George Westinghouse passed away in New York City on March 12, 1914, at age 67. Although the two men had moved on to different projects after their business partnership ended, Tesla always had profound respect for the man who, by acquiring Tesla's patents, had been able to build, market, and introduce the components of the Tesla polyphase alternating current system to the world.

**Nikola Tesla Corner at Sixth Avenue and West 40th Street in Manhattan, New York.** *Wikimedia Commons*

Without Westinghouse's involvement, it's possible that Tesla's AC system might have gone the way of some of his other undeveloped ideas and inventions. The Tesla-Westinghouse team undeniably changed the course of electrical history, and Tesla said of his late benefactor, "His was a wonderful career filled with remarkable achievements. He gave to the world a number of valuable inventions and improvements, created new industries, advanced the mechanical and electrical arts and improved in many ways the conditions of modern life. He was a great pioneer and builder whose work was of far-reaching effect on his time and whose name will live long in the memory of men."

## The Great War and Early Superweapon Ideas

The year also brought death to many more men, as 1914 marked the beginning of the Great War, which would later be referred to as World War I. In fact, the whole bloody ordeal began in Tesla's homeland of the Balkans. On June 28, 1914, the heir to the Astro-Hungarian throne, Archduke Franz Ferdinand, and his wife, Sophie, were assassinated in the Bosnian city of Sarajevo by a Bosnian-Serb revolutionary. This act led to a convoluted untangling of alliances and declarations of war involving many countries. Before long, the Great War was raging across Europe. The United States would not enter the fray until 1917; after German U-boats torpedoed three American ships, President Woodrow Wilson persuaded Congress to declare war on Germany.

Many Americans had probably never heard of Bosnia or the Balkans before the Great War, but much of Tesla's family still lived in the area and would be affected. It's very possible that the outbreak of this war may have been the catalyst for one of his most mysterious invention concepts, "a weapon of sufficient magnitude" that could end the war quickly. On December 20, 1914, Tesla published an article in the *New York Sun* titled, "Nikola Tesla Looks to Science to End the War." He would continue to work on and promote this idea for what would later be called a death ray over the next three decades, but his main motivation would always be to bring an end to war.

## The Nobel Prize Puzzle and the Edison Medal

In November 1915, the *New York Times* announced that Nikola Tesla and Thomas Edison were to share the Nobel Prize in Physics. Both men reported that they'd received no official notification of the award, but Tesla was excited that his contributions in wireless communication transmission might finally be recognized. He was still very bitter that Marconi had won the prize in 1909 and hoped to set the record straight.

It's true that both men perhaps deserved to win a Nobel Prize, but unfortunately, the newspaper got it wrong. One week later, the Nobel Prize Committee announced that father and son British scientists Sir William Henry Bragg and William Lawrence Bragg were awarded the Nobel Prize in Physics for their work with X-rays and crystals.

What a disappointment for Tesla, as he could've certainly used the $20,000 prize money. As usual, his financial state was poor, and by 1916 he was forced to declare bankruptcy.

On March 16, 1916, a humiliating article appeared in the *New York World* entitled "Tesla No Money Wizard; Swamped by Debts, He Vows." The article gave details of Tesla's appearance and testimony in a state Supreme Court hearing, stating that he lived in the Waldorf on credit and had no money or assets with which to pay his debts. But Tesla did not know that his statements would be written in a newspaper article for all to see. He was mortified. Moreover, he'd already lost the deed to Wardenclyffe, which caused him even more shame and disappointment.

Biographer Marc J. Seifer noted that this event was a turning point in Tesla's life. Seifer stated that the inventor now felt that "the world had officially branded him a dud. If success is measured in a material way, it was clear that Tesla was the ultimate failure." Also, Tesla's superstar status had dulled over the years, and many people had forgotten all about his breakthrough work with AC power. So, although Tesla kept up appearances, "he began the slow but steady turning away from society."

Ironically, Tesla was nominated for an award in 1917, which was named in honor of Thomas Edison and presented by the American Institute of Electrical Engineers. Bernard A. Behrend, vice president of the institute, was a Swiss immigrant who had long respected Tesla and admired his work. In fact, Behrend had written one of the earliest textbooks on AC motors. He also wanted to help restore Tesla's reputation, and he was the one who suggested to the AIEE committee that Nikola Tesla should receive the Edison Medal. Past winners were Alexander Graham Bell, Elihu Thomson, and George Westinghouse.

When Tesla first found out that he'd won the Edison Medal, he wanted no part of it. He refused to accept the honor. Why would he want an award named for his greatest competitor? Behrend then appealed to the inventor's pride and asked if he really wanted to turn down the opportunity to be recognized as the creator of the AC power system and other important inventions. At this, Tesla agreed, and the award ceremony was scheduled for May 18, 1917.

According to legend, Tesla became so nervous that he left the building during the opening speech. How embarrassing to Behrend and the ceremony's organizers! Without the guest of honor, they could not continue. Tesla's first biographer, John J. O'Neill, wrote that Behrend finally found the inventor nearby, standing in the plaza in front of the New York Public Library. Tesla was "wearing a crown of two pigeons on his head, his shoulders and arms festooned with a dozen more, their white or pale-blue bodies making strong contrast with his black suit and black hair, even in the dusk. On either side of his outstretched hands was another bird, while seemingly hundreds more made a living carpet on the ground in front of him, hopping about and pecking at the bird seed he had been scattering."

As the story goes, Behrend appealed to Tesla not to let him down. He graciously asked the inventor to return to the auditorium to receive his award.

Although Tesla would seemingly have been more comfortable staying at the library's plaza with his feathered friends, he agreed. His disappearance had delayed the ceremony by 20 minutes. Moreover, Tesla had not prepared a formal acceptance speech, so he simply recounted the principles of his original polyphase AC system for his audience.

When Behrend presented the Edison Medal to Tesla that evening, part of his speech included these words: "We asked Mr. Tesla to accept this medal. We did not do this for the mere sake . . . of perpetuating a name . . . for so long as men occupy themselves with our industry . . . the name of Tesla runs no more risk of oblivion than does that of Faraday, or that of Edison."

Behrend sincerely meant these words, as he truly believed Tesla's work and name would never fade from society's consciousness. Unfortunately, Behrend's prediction would prove to be untrue, but on that spring night in New York City, Tesla and his achievements were honored. And after so many recent disappointments, perhaps the award did help the inventor feel that all his accomplishments had not been completely forgotten by his peers. Biographer Margaret Cheney wrote that Tesla kept his Edison Medal in his safe for the rest of his life, and that it was one of his most treasured possessions. She also noted that the medal disappeared after his death and has never been recovered.

## More Wardenclyffe Woes

Ever since Nikola Tesla had signed over the Wardenclyffe deed to the Waldorf-Astoria's manager, George C. Boldt, to clear up his hotel bills, ideas had been tossed around about what to do with the buildings. Suggestions included repurposing the site for a pickle factory or letting the War Department use the property. Nothing was ever done, and in the end, the threat of German spies using the site during World War I led the US government to destroy the Wardenclyffe tower—or at least, that was the rumor.

The logical and more widely accepted explanation is that the Waldorf-Astoria hotel corporation hired a salvage company to dynamite the tower on July 4, 1917, for scrap metal. In truth, Tesla had always assumed that he'd regain the deed to the Wardenclyffe property from Boldt once he had the money to pay off his hotel debts. Therefore, he was understandably devastated to find out what had happened on the site of his most cherished dream.

Sadly, the magnificent Wardenclyffe tower was destroyed, but the stately brick laboratory was left deserted for many years. In 2012, the organization Friends of Science East purchased the property with plans to restore the lab and eventually open a museum called the Tesla Science Center at Wardenclyffe. Although the center is not yet fully operational, the property was listed on the National Register of Historic Places in 2018.

## Consulting Jobs and Writing an Autobiography

Tesla moved to Chicago, Illinois, in the summer of 1917 to work with Pyle-National Company to perfect his bladeless turbine. As was his norm for

# WRITE YOUR AUTOBIOGRAPHY

*An autobiography is the written account of a person's life, written by the person. Tesla's autobiography is fascinating to read, especially the parts about his childhood and early adult years. He wrote it in installments for a magazine in 1919, but today you can find it as a book.*

*Why not record your own life story thus far? Even if you're young, your experiences, memories, and thoughts are worth recording. It will be fun to read back over what you write when you are older.*

## You'll Need

⚡ Hardbound journal

⚡ Paper and pen

⚡ Stickers, markers, paints, memorabilia, photos (optional)

1. Collect factual information about your life: birth and family information, early years, memories, activities, sports, awards, honors, and anything that you feel is important.

2. Write your autobiography, starting at the beginning.

3. As you describe events in your life, add photos, memorabilia, or original artwork.

4. Keep your autobiography, and add to it through the years.

enjoying gracious hotel living, he stayed at the Blackstone Hotel for 16 months, until November 1918. Upon his return to New York City, he moved into Room 1607 at the St. Regis hotel. After 20 years of living (and accruing many debts) at the Waldorf-Astoria prior to his stay in Chicago, he knew it was time to make a change.

Although Tesla now considered the St. Regis his permanent residence, he was away from New York City a good bit of the time from 1917 until 1926. After his stint with the Pyle-National Company, he also consulted or worked with the Allis-Chalmers Manufacturing Company in Milwaukee, Wisconsin; the Waltham Watch Company in Boston, Massachusetts; and the Budd Company in Philadelphia, Pennsylvania.

Additionally, Tesla wrote articles for *Electrical Experimenter* magazine to help supplement his meager income. One specific article explained his vision for radar, using electromagnetic waves to detect ships. He also kept improving old inventions and worked on developing new ones. During this time, he produced a speedometer, a tachometer, and a motor used in motion picture equipment. He even developed and sold a "fluid flow tube," which could not only pump oil from the ground but also be attached to the bladeless turbine to turn it into a combustion engine.

Tesla used his days for work, but during his nights in Chicago he began to write his autobiography in a series of articles. These were also published in the *Electrical Experimenter* throughout 1919. The autobiographical articles provided many of the details of Tesla's early childhood,

teen, college, and young adult years in the Balkans and Europe that were later used by others to write biographies of the quirky inventor.

Author Marc J. Seifer noted that the stories from Tesla's early years "oozed charm and wit, with [their] numerous Mark Twainian depictions of amusing anecdotes, harrowing experiences, life with his inventive mother, preacher father, prodigal brother, and three doting sisters."

So, were these incidents and events depicting "an unusual tale of a wizard-child growing up in another era in a faraway land" possibly dramatized or slightly exaggerated? Only Tesla knew for sure, but his exciting written accounts about his life and inventions are interesting to readers even today.

## Bizarre Behavior, Pigeon Problems, and Hotel Hassles

Through the 1920s and early '30s, Tesla tried to live off the small royalties from his newer inventions and money earned from consulting and writing. But since he was used to lavish living and dining, this was not always easy. He was also sad that his close friends Robert and Katharine Johnson had moved to Italy in 1920, where Robert had been appointed US ambassador. Additionally, some of Tesla's other friends and former loyal supporters had died or turned their backs on him.

The inventor's reclusive and already strange behavior seemed to become even more bizarre. He walked around the city for hours each night, and he spent more and more time in the company of the pigeons he fed. He would take sick or injured birds back to his hotel room to care for them, and many other pigeons would land on the sill of his open hotel window as well. The hotel staff and maids began to complain about the birdseed and droppings in Tesla's room, but he kept on taking care of his feathered friends despite the objections.

Tesla especially loved one pure-white female pigeon with gray-tipped wings. He said that she gave him joy and purpose—and that no matter where he was, she would find him. When he wanted her, he only had to wish and call her, and she would come flying to him. He also claimed that one night as he lay in his bed in the dark, this beloved pigeon flew through his open window because she needed him. Tesla got up and went to the window. He later recounted, "As I looked at her I knew she wanted to tell me—she was dying. And then, as I got her message, there came a light from her eyes—powerful beams of light. . . . When that pigeon died, something went out of my life. . . . I knew my life's work was finished."

Tesla's experience and obsession with pigeons is puzzling, and historians and psychologists have debated the meaning of his bizarre claim about the dying pigeon since the story was recorded in 1922. But the odd phenomena of the beams of light that Tesla said he saw coming from the pigeon's eyes calls to mind his strange revelation about his AC motor as the blazing sun was setting in the Budapest park years before or the other unexplainable visions accompanied by flashes of light during his childhood. Perhaps all these peculiar experiences were simply the way the highly sensitive inventor *perceived* the events as they occurred.

A white pigeon, like the one that was Tesla's favorite. *Tesla Universe*

Whatever the case, Tesla cared greatly for his feathered friends, especially the pigeons in Bryant Park near the New York Public Library. Visitors to the city today will see a sign at one end of the park, at the corner of Sixth Avenue and West 40th Street, that designates the spot as NIKOLA TESLA CORNER in his honor.

Despite his gentle nature with animals, Tesla inevitably ran into trouble at the St. Regis. The management and staff finally had enough of pigeons in Tesla's room and seeds and droppings on windowsills and floors. Too, he'd incurred over $3,000 in charges in only seven months. He was unable to pay the bill, so in 1923 he took his leave of the hotel and moved to the elegant and luxurious Hotel Marguery at 270 Park Avenue.

**Postcard from the New Yorker Hotel, where Tesla spent the last years of his life.** *Author's collection*

Unfortunately, Tesla did nothing about trying to repay his debts to the St. Regis, and within six months he was being sued by the hotel for the balance he owed. A law enforcement officer was even sent to the inventor's office to confiscate all the furniture in order to satisfy the debt, but Tesla somehow talked him into waiting.

In reality, the only thing he owned of any worth was his Edison Medal locked in the safe. He was even weeks behind in paying his secretaries, and he had no money in the bank. When he did discover $5.00 in an office drawer, he instructed his secretary to buy bird feed with the money! Not long after this episode, Tesla moved his office space to Madison Avenue, where he worked for the next few years.

Tesla kept his room at the Hotel Marguery until 1925, but he also secured another room at the Hotel Pennsylvania to use as his main residence for some reason during part of this time. He continued to live at the Hotel Pennsylvania for a few more years until his debts and pigeon friends became problems again. Next, he relocated to the Hotel Governor Clinton, but after about a year, the other residents began to complain about Tesla's pigeons, so the management asked him to leave. He finally ended up at the New Yorker Hotel in Manhattan in 1933. This would be his home for the last ten years of his life.

## Honors and Family Ties

Although Tesla never graduated from a university, he was not forgotten by the institutions of higher learning in his native land. In June 1926, he received honorary doctorate degrees from both the University of Belgrade and the University of Zagreb. Most of Tesla's fellow countrymen considered him a national hero, even in his old age, and they were proud of his many accomplishments. Bestowing honorary degrees on him was one way to show their continued support. Additionally, during his last few years, the Yugoslav government gave him $7,200 a year to help provide for his immediate needs.

Family was always important to Tesla, even though he rarely saw his sisters after he immigrated to America. But in 1926 he met his nephew, Sava Kosanović, for the very first time when the younger man visited New York City. Sava, the son of Nikola's youngest sister, Marica, later became Yugoslavia's first ambassador to the United States. He'd heard all about his famous uncle while growing up, and he would also play an important part in Tesla's last years—and in events after his death.

# Celebrating 75

According to biographer Margaret Cheney, Tesla rarely took notice of his birthdays during his early years, but as he got older, the yearly anniversaries became more important to the reclusive inventor. Tesla used these celebratory occasions to meet with reporters and photographers and discuss his latest inventions and prophecies, and he always enjoyed the attention he received.

In July 1931, a young science writer and friend, Kenneth Swezey, organized a 75th birthday celebration of sorts for Tesla. Swezey asked prominent scientists, engineers, and inventors from all over the world to send congratulatory letters or tributes to the aging Tesla, and more than 70 people responded. This group included famous men such as Albert Einstein, Sir Oliver Lodge, Lee De Forest, Robert Millikan, and even Sir William Henry Bragg, who along with his son had won the 1915 Nobel Prize in Physics that had reportedly first belonged to Tesla and Edison. Each man "acknowledged with respect and gratitude, [Tesla's] inspiration in their own careers." Unsurprisingly, Guglielmo Marconi declined to send a birthday greeting.

Thanks to Kenneth Swezey's influence, magazines and newspapers all over the world carried articles about Tesla to commemorate his 75th birthday. And along with a feature article, *Time* magazine even showcased on its July 20, 1931, cover his *Blue Portrait*, painted by Princess Vilma Lwoff-Parlaghy of Hungary 15 years earlier.

Swezey felt that Tesla was secretly pleased by the attention and letters he received, although the inventor did act a bit indifferent when he was presented with a bound volume of the tributes and compliments from some of his former opponents. In fact, when Swezey later asked Tesla if he could temporarily borrow the letters to make copies to send to the Tesla Institute at Belgrade (now the Nikola Tesla Institute of Electrical Engineering at the University of Belgrade), the older man was hesitant to part with them.

During his birthday interviews, Tesla told reporters about a new form of energy he'd discovered. *Time* magazine reported his words: "When I say a new *source*, I mean that I have turned for power to a source which no previous scientist has turned, to the best of my knowledge. . . . It will throw light on many puzzling phenomena of the cosmos, and may prove also of great industrial value. . . . I can only say at this time it will come from an entirely new and unsuspected source, and will be for all practical purposes constant day and night, and at all times of the year. The apparatus . . . will be of ideal simplicity."

But when asked when he'd give a formal announcement of this discovery, Tesla politely evaded giving a definitive answer by responding with "in a few months, or a few years."

The *Time* article's writer went on to say, "It is improbable that he will ever design such a device on paper, let alone in a machine shop, although before his mind's eye he may see it in every detail, motion, and defect. He is a great visualizer."

Announcing his latest ideas, then declining to give specific details became the norm in Tesla's later years. And while it's true that he visualized more inventions and ideas than he ever actually created, no one could deny his talent and amazing mind. Moreover, the aging genius had to be encouraged and pleased by the attention, birthday wishes, and accolades he received. Perhaps this 75th birthday celebration motivated Tesla to keep going—and to keep dreaming.

# DESIGN A MAGAZINE COVER

*Think about the magazine issues you've read or seen online or on display in stores. Do the front covers have catchy titles, graphics, art, headlines for articles covered inside, and colorful text? Does the main graphic of the person or subject on the magazine cover stir your interest?*

*Try your hand at a creating a magazine cover featuring a famous person—past or present.*

## You'll Need

⚡ Magazines

⚡ Library or internet access

⚡ Paper and art supplies

⚡ Scissors

⚡ Glue

⚡ Computer with design software (optional)

1. Study the covers of different magazines—at home, in a library, or online. Note the colors, headlines, date and issue numbers, etc. What do you like most about the covers? What do you like least?

2. Brainstorm ideas and subjects for your cover. Decide on the person you want to feature. Jot down the things or accomplishments that make this person famous or well known.

3. Sketch out a few ideas for your cover and decide which version would work best. Get creative! Be sure to include the magazine title, subheadings that tell more about your famous person and his/her accomplishments, a large graphic of the person, date, issue number, and anything else you feel is important.

4. Use paper and art supplies to create your final cover. If you are familiar with design software, create it on a computer and print it out.

**Science News**

DECEMBER 1911
vol. 5, no. 12

**Marie Curie**

TWO-TIME WINNER OF THE
NOBEL PRIZE TELLS ALL!

+ Her triumphs and tragedies
+ Balancing life and work
+ Her childhood in Poland
+ Her future

**Also in this issue:**
RADIUM CURES: QUACK OR REAL?
JOHN JOSEPH RAWLINGS FILES UK PATENT FOR WALL PLUG
WILL ROALD AMUNDSEN REACH THE SOUTH POLE?

# QUIET DEPARTURES

---

*Tesla's mind was a human dynamo that whirled to benefit mankind.*
—Col. David Sarnoff, president of RCA

---

Throughout his life, Nikola Tesla usually pondered mind-blowing plans and ideas. But he also had more practical concerns, such as protecting the environment and conserving natural resources. In December 1931, *Everyday Science and Mechanics* magazine printed an article entitled "Our Future Motive Power" outlining Tesla's ideas for solving the "problem of obtaining power to replace our wasted fuel and [indicating] the method of tapping the earth's hidden resources which will support the industry of future generations." The article also featured two detailed designs with illustrations—one for extracting electricity from seawater and another for a geothermal steam plant.

**Nikola Tesla monument in Prague, Czech Republic.** *Author's collection*

Tesla's research into these alternate sources of power were merely preliminary, but the concepts were ones he'd mulled over for years. Of course, Tesla never lived to see these ideas realized. Yet, he predicted that any of the "technical problems could be solved and that one day such [steam] plants would be major producers of power." And as biographer Margaret Cheney noted, "As is typical of so many of Tesla's inventions, scholars still do not know the whole range of their possible applications or, in some cases, even their full theoretical significance."

Tesla also had opinions about what the world would be like in the future. He correctly predicted that humans would begin to see the dangers of pollution and unclean water—and that measures would be taken to find more ways to keep the earth clean. He also believed that unhealthy products, such as tobacco, would become less popular. Unfortunately, his belief that scientists would find ways to "end droughts, forest fires, and floods" has not been realized yet.

## The Westinghouse Corporation Comes Through

As always, Tesla still struggled to manage financially. Yet, according to Hugo Gernsback, one of Tesla's most loyal admirers and editor of the *Electrical Experimenter*, the elderly inventor was a very proud man. It's true that Tesla had no qualms about living on credit, signing collateral notes for inventions or working models of ideas, because he felt he had something valuable he could exchange.

But he would not accept outright charity under any circumstance. Therefore, Gernsback stepped in to see if he could help Tesla find some sort of honorary consulting position that would provide him with a small salary.

It's possible that Gernsback even appealed to the Westinghouse Corporation with this special request, because in early 1934, the company consented to help "their former champion out" by paying him $125 a month as a consulting engineer. The Westinghouse Corporation also came to an agreement with the New Yorker Hotel, which allowed Tesla to live there rent free for the rest of his life. With the $7,200 yearly stipend he received from Yugoslavia, Tesla was able to survive. And even though he really couldn't afford it, he always gave "generous tips to those who had rendered him the slightest assistance and handouts" or "to anyone he thought was in need."

## Particle Beam Weapon

In the early summer of 1934, Tesla received the John Scott Medal from the city of Philadelphia for his invention of the rotating magnetic field and the induction motor. It was a well-deserved honor. But a bit of sensationalism was soon to follow. After his 75th birthday celebration, Tesla had begun granting interviews to the press each year on his birthday, and in July 1934 he certainly got the attention of reporters. Although rumors and speculation about his so-called death ray had been going on since the beginning of World War I, the 78-year-old Tesla dropped a bombshell announcement. He claimed that he'd been perfecting a particle beam weapon, one that would make any country, of any size, safe from enemy attacks on ground or from the air.

Influenced by his father, Tesla did not believe in violence. His dream was to end war, and he believed he'd found the answer for peace. But more than once, he had to emphasize to reporters that his invention was not actually a death ray. Rays diffused over distance. No, his apparatus used charged particle beams "which may be relatively large or of microscopic dimensions, enabling us to convey to a small area at a great distance of trillions of times more energy than is possible with rays of any kind. Many thousands of horsepower can thus be transmitted by a stream thinner than a hair, so that nothing can resist."

Tesla initially approached Jack Morgan, J. P. Morgan's son, to see if he would be interested in financing a prototype of the particle beam weapon, since he had previously given money to help develop the bladeless turbine. Tesla told Morgan he figured it would take about three months to build and cost around $2 million. But Morgan, facing his own financial problems due to the Great Depression, couldn't tell if the inventor "was talking sense or nonsense." He passed on the opportunity.

Over the next three years, almost everyone realized that another war was inevitable, and this was the very thing Tesla had hoped to avoid with the apparatus that he often referred to as his "peace beam." His theory remained that "if no country [could] be attacked successfully, there [would] be no purpose in war."

## TESLA'S ANNOUNCEMENT MADE THE NEWS

The *New York Times* reported on July 11, 1934, that Tesla claimed "the apparatus could send concentrated beams of particles through the free air, of such tremendous energy that they will bring down a fleet of 10,000 enemy airplanes at a distance of 250 miles from a defending nation's border and will cause armies of millions to drop dead in their tracks."

He also said his new weapon would end war, because his beam "would surround each country like an invisible Chinese wall, only a million times more impenetrable." It could only be used defensively, however, and not as an offensive weapon. Moreover, he explained that the beam "could be generated only from large, stationary and immovable power plants, stationed in the manner of old-time forts at various strategic distances from each country's border. They could not be moved for the purposes of attack."

**An artist's rendering of how Tesla's death beam could bring down 10,000 enemy planes within a 250-mile radius.** *Tesla Universe*

# SOLAR OVEN S'MORES

*Nikola Tesla was always looking for ways to use renewable energy resources, and of course, the sun is the most powerful energy resource of all. In this activity, you will make a solar oven and harness the sun's energy to make some s'mores!*

--------------------------------------------------------------------------------

**ADULT SUPERVISION REQUIRED**

## You'll Need

⚡ Clean, empty cardboard pizza box (medium size works well)

⚡ Ruler

⚡ Pen or pencil

⚡ Scissors or utility craft knife

⚡ Aluminum foil

⚡ Glue

⚡ Clear plastic wrap

⚡ Strong tape

⚡ Black construction paper

⚡ S'more ingredients: graham crackers, large marshmallows, chocolate bars

⚡ Wooden skewer

1. On the pizza box top, measure and draw three 10½-inch (27-centimeter) lines, two from the back fold and one connecting the other two. You are creating a hinged "door flap," so leave the back edge of the flap attached to the pizza box. Ask an adult to help you cut along the lines you drew with scissors or a craft knife.

2. Cover the underside of the flap you just made with aluminum foil and glue in place.

3. Open the remaining frame of the box top and stretch a piece of clear plastic wrap across the underside of the opening you just cut out. Attach the wrap with tape.

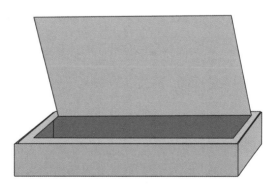

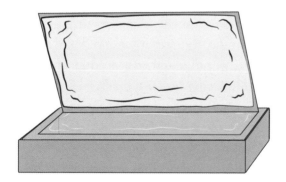

4. Cover the bottom of the inside of the box with black construction paper and glue in place.

5. Build your s'mores—graham cracker on the bottom, then a square of chocolate, topped with a marshmallow. Place the s'mores on the black paper inside of the box and close the clear plastic wrap lid over them.

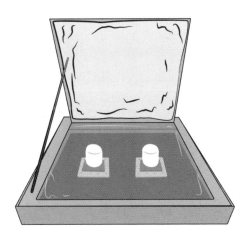

6. Prop open the aluminum foil flap with a wooden skewer. Position the solar oven so the sun's rays reflect down on the s'mores for about 30–60 minutes, or until the chocolate and marshmallows are soft and melted.

7. Remove the s'mores and enjoy!

Tesla was frustrated that he'd not been able to find anyone to finance his idea, so he tried another tactic. He wrote a technical paper with elaborate diagrams, titled "New Art of Projecting Concentrated Non-Dispersive Energy Through Natural Media," and sent his proposal to several nations hoping to generate interest. Although he did correspond with a few national leaders, including British prime minister Neville Chamberlain, nothing ever materialized. But the plan and paper must've piqued the interest of J. Edgar Hoover, head of the FBI, as it has been alleged that he began keeping a file on Tesla at that time.

Eventually the Soviet Union showed interest in the particle beam weapon, and Tesla entered into negotiations with Soviet representatives in April 1935. In return for $25,000, Tesla was to "supply plans, specifications, and complete information on a method and apparatus" for his particle beam weapon. Apparently "Soviet scientists and engineers studied Tesla's plans and corresponded with him further, but we do not know whether the Soviets tested such a device in the 1930s."

During the time of his negotiations with the Soviets, Tesla claimed that spies broke into his hotel room and went through his papers with the intention of stealing the specific particle beam weapon plans. They were unsuccessful, Tesla later told biographer John J. O'Neill, because he only carried the key details around in his head, instead of putting them down on paper.

Since his death, biographers have speculated as to whether Tesla built a prototype of the death ray or not. Reputable witnesses reported that he did produce some working models along the lines of the apparatus he described, and Tesla himself claimed that he had built, demonstrated, and used it. Indeed he had two secret laboratories throughout the 1930s that reporters were never allowed to enter, so it's possible that Tesla at least attempted to construct parts of his particle beam weapon. Historians agree that it's a question that will never be fully answered.

When World War II began, Tesla once again approached the US government, offering the service of all his inventions, including the particle beam weapon, which he considered his gift to mankind. He sent word that he was ready to go to work for America and continue for as long as he was able. But Tesla stated that if the government accepted his offer, there would be stipulations. He would not tolerate interference from any experts—and federal officials would have to trust him. Unsurprisingly, he did not hear back from them.

Tesla never saw his particle beam weapon put to use in World War II, but during the Cold War (after his death), both the United States and USSR worked on charged particle beam weapons. He summed it up nicely in his interview and article in the February 1935 issue of *Liberty* magazine when he said, "It seems that I have always been ahead of my time." And indeed, he was.

Tesla receives awards from Czechoslovakia and Yugoslavia at a reception in his honor in New York on July 10, 1937. *Tesla Universe*

## Honors and Injuries

Tesla received 13 honorary doctorate degrees in his lifetime, including three in 1937 from the University of Poitiers, the University of France, and the University of Prague. He also was decorated with the Order of the White Lion, the highest order or distinction given to a foreign citizen by Czechoslovakia. Yugoslavia followed suit by bestowing upon him its highest order, the Grand Cordon of the White Eagle, as well. Both awards were presented at a luncheon in honor of his 81st birthday.

According to biographer Marc J. Seifer, Tesla looked "much like an eagle himself, with his long, hawk-shaped proboscis [nose] accentuated by his extreme leanness." After the luncheon, the inventor entertained a group of reporters in his hotel suite, where he "read a prepared treatise outlining his latest inventions and plans for contacting nearby planets."

In January, Tesla had also been notified that he was elected to full membership in the Serbian Royal Academy. Founded in 1886, it was the most prominent academic institution in Serbia. This was a bittersweet honor, as he'd originally not been accepted into this prestigious organization at an earlier date, even though he was the first scientist ever nominated for permanent membership.

Unfortunately, Tesla also suffered a serious injury that same year. One August evening, he left his hotel around midnight to begin his usual round of feeding the pigeons. But as the 81-year-old inventor crossed the street, he was hit by a taxicab and fell to the ground, where he lay for some time. Then, refusing help, he rose to his feet and slowly made his way back to his hotel room. He immediately called William Kerrigan, his favorite messenger boy at the Postal Telegraph Company (later Western Union), to come and feed the pigeons. Then he collapsed on his bed. He later claimed that the accident only caused bruises and upset his digestion a bit, but other sources report he wrenched his back and suffered three broken ribs. Whatever the true extent of his injuries, he was bedridden for the next six months. He was often feverish, and he battled several bouts of pneumonia.

Three important people in Tesla's life died in 1937, one a rival and two close friends. Richmond P. Hobson died on March 16, 1937; Guglielmo Marconi died on July 20, 1937; and Robert Underwood Johnson passed away on October 14, 1937. Although elderly, weak, and sick himself, the deaths of these three men would've undoubtedly upset the inventor.

Most of the people Tesla had socialized with, competed against, or worked with were now gone. The world he now lived in had changed so much from the one he'd once known.

## Generosity for the Long-Departed Twain

Unsurprisingly, Tesla's overall health declined rapidly, and his appearance became even more skeletal as he lost more weight. His diet consisted almost exclusively of warm milk and crackers. Also, his thoughts became very irrational at times. In fact, one morning not long before he died, he asked William Kerrigan to deliver a sealed envelope as quickly as possible to Mr. Samuel Clemens at 35 South Fifth Avenue.

Kerrigan came back a short while later and reported to Tesla that there was no *South* Fifth Avenue, and he could find no one on Fifth Avenue by the name of Clemens. Tesla became irritated. He explained that Samuel Clemens was the writer, Mark Twain, and that he did indeed live on South Fifth Avenue—and Kerrigan needed to go back and deliver that letter immediately!

Kerrigan left again, but this time he stopped and told his manager at the Postal Telegraph Company about his dilemma. The manager said, "Of course you couldn't find South Fifth Avenue. Its name was changed to West Broadway years ago, and you won't be able to deliver a message to Mark Twain because he has been dead for twenty-five years." It had actually been 28 years, as Clemens died in 1910.

When Kerrigan explained to Tesla what had happened, the old man was further confused and upset. He denied that Twain was dead. He was adamant that his dear friend had visited him the night before and needed financial help. Tesla insisted that the boy go to another location to deliver the letter, but it was the address of Tesla's first laboratory. Unsure of what to do, Kerrigan and his manager opened the sealed envelope to look for clues as to where to deliver the envelope. They discovered 20 $5 bills folded up in a blank sheet of paper. Kerrigan tried to return the money to Tesla, but the annoyed inventor told the boy to either deliver the money or keep it.

## Absentee Honoree

In May 1938, the National Institute of Immigrant Welfare held an award ceremony in honor of Tesla and two other recipients, Felix Frankfurter of Harvard Law School and Giovanni Martinelli of the Metropolitan Opera, at the Biltmore Hotel in New York City. This was to be one of his final honors, but Tesla was unable to attend the ceremony due to his health. Dr. Paul Radosavljevich, a professor at New York University, accepted Tesla's honor on his behalf and read the speech the inventor had prepared and sent in his absence. Apparently, Tesla still harbored deep resentment toward the late Thomas Edison, as the speech included the story of Edison's false (or joking) promise to pay Tesla $50,000 if he could improve the DC generators in his power stations.

Why did Tesla choose Dr. Radosavljevich to attend the ceremony and accept the award on his behalf? They were friends, and the professor obviously wanted to help the aging inventor. But they shared another connection that was quite disturbing as well. It seems they were both eugenicists who supported the idea that the quality of the human race could be improved through selective breeding. They thought it was appropriate to discourage (or force) parents whom they considered to be inferior with undesirable traits from reproducing, while encouraging other parents, whom they felt were superior with desirable traits, to have children.

That Tesla would have had such ideas is disappointing and troubling. He was so generous and kind in other ways, yet certainly misguided in his beliefs in this area. But as writer Matt Novak stated in an article published for the Smithsonian website, "The inventor may have been brilliant . . . [but] he was still just human."

## War Tension

World War II military tensions began to rise in and around the Balkans and Yugoslavia, and Tesla was very upset and often confused about what was happening in his homeland and to his former countrymen. To ward off a German attack,

Yugoslavia's regent, Prince Paul, had accepted a compromise from Adolf Hitler and agreed to unite the country with the Axis Powers. The Axis Powers was an alliance of the German and Austro-Hungarian Empires, and later it also included the Ottoman Empire and the Kingdom of Bulgaria.

The Yugoslavian citizens were very angry with this decision and worked together to overthrow and replace the regent. Their choice, King Peter II, the 17-year-old son of the former king Alexander, ascended the throne as monarch on March 28, 1941. Tesla was pleased, as he'd long admired the new king's late father. The inventor had been a loyal American citizen for many years, but he still cared deeply about the people he'd left behind in his old country.

Not long after these events, Sava Kosanović arrived in New York and began helping to take care of his ailing uncle. But American government officials suspected Kosanović of having ties to the Communist party. Unbeknownst to Tesla, Sava was writing and sending statements to encourage the people of Yugoslavia and the Soviet Academy of Sciences in their "revolutionary struggle," which was supported by the USSR. And Sava was signing Tesla's name! As biographer Margaret Cheney noted, the elderly man had no idea that he was being used for Communist propaganda.

When King Peter and his government refused to follow through with Prince Paul's agreement with Hitler, the Germans began bombing Yugoslavia's capital of Belgrade, killing thousands of citizens and destroying most of the city. The newly built Tesla Institute also lay in ruins. The German

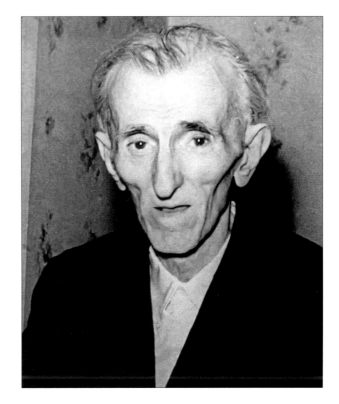

**Probably the last photo of Nikola Tesla taken before his death.** *Tesla Universe*

armies then invaded the country, but King Peter escaped to England, where he would operate his government for the rest of the war. He did, however, visit the United States in 1942 to meet with Franklin D. Roosevelt, seeking help for his exiled Yugoslav monarchist government. King Peter's visit with FDR was unsuccessful. The United States had already pledged support to the Yugoslav Communist government, which had risen under the command of Josip Tito after Peter fled from Yugoslavia, in hopes of defeating Nazi Germany.

But Peter did get to visit with Tesla during his US trip, and the young king was delighted to meet the hero of his homeland. In his diaries, *A King's Heritage*, he wrote:

# IT'S A BUST

*Tesla met Ivan Meštrović, a talented and famous Croatian sculptor, architect, and writer, when he visited New York City in 1924. The two became good friends, and in 1939, Tesla requested that the sculptor create a bust of him. A bust is a sculpture of a person's head, shoulders, and chest. Meštrović agreed, and the original plaster model can still be seen at the Croatian Academy of Art and Science in Zagreb, Croatia.*

*Try to make a bust of someone famous—or even yourself—out of papier-mâché. The word papier-mâché is French for "chewed paper."*

## You'll Need

⚡ Round balloon

⚡ Scissors

⚡ Rectangular cardboard box for the base, 8 by 6 by 10 inches (20 by 15 by 25 centimeters) works well

⚡ Tape

⚡ Paper towel roll cardboard tube

⚡ 1 cup (120 grams) flour

⚡ 2 cups (237 milliliters) cold water

⚡ Mixing bowl

⚡ Duct tape

⚡ Whisk

⚡ Old newspapers or brown paper bags cut into 1-inch (3-centimeter) strips

⚡ Paintbrush, acrylic paints, markers, spray paint, etc.

1. Blow up and tie off a balloon. It should be the size of a human head.

2. Using scissors, poke a hole in the center of a rectangular box for a base. Push the tied end of the balloon through the hole and tape it to the underside of the box.

3. Support the "head" using a paper towel tube: Cut it in half the short way, then in half horizontally to create "shoulders." Place the shoulder pieces on either side of the balloon, and tape in place.

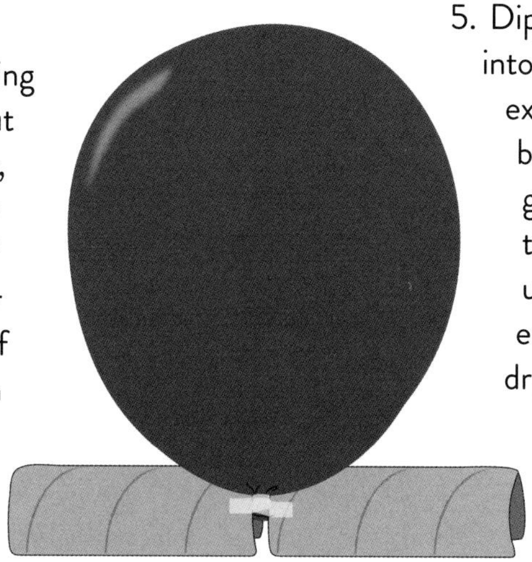

4. Mix 1 cup (120 grams) flour and 2 cups (237 milliliters) water in a bowl with a whisk until smooth. The paste should be thin and runny like glue. If it's thick, add a bit more water. If it's too thin, add a bit more flour.

5. Dip newspaper or paper strips into the paste, removing the excess by running the strips between two pinched fingers. Spread the strips over the balloon, tubes, and base until covered. Apply several layers, but let each layer dry completely before adding another.

6. Shape facial features such as eyes, eye-brows, nose, lips, and ears, and add hair with additional papier-mâché, letting each feature dry completely between layers.

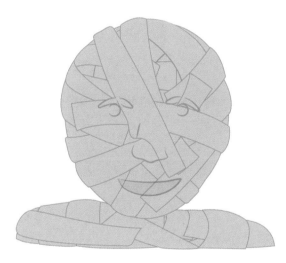

7. Once the bust is dry, spray paint it one color to look like metal (such as copper or bronze) or use art materials to paint it with more life-like colors. The choice is up to you!

**Bust of Nikola Tesla created by Ivan Meštrović in 1939.** *Tesla Universe*

# KING PETER II OF YUGOSLAVIA

King Peter II was the last monarch of Yugoslavia, and his short reign marked the end of Karađorđević dynasty rulers. He was born on September 6, 1923, in Belgrade (now in Serbia) to Alexander I and Queen Maria of Yugoslavia and called Crown Prince Peter. His godfather was King George V of England.

Alexander I's kingdom had been created right after World War I by the Paris Peace Conference. It was made up of several divided or combined countries, so there was a lot of tension and political unrest.

Alexander's rule was difficult, and many did not agree with his decisions. During a state visit to Marseille, France, on October 9, 1934, he was assassinated by a Macedonian revolutionary who was part of group that wanted to secede from Yugoslavia. It was the first assassination ever captured on film, as a cameraman happened to be close by when it happened.

Peter was only 11 when his father was killed, and he became king. Because of his young age, however, his cousin, Prince Paul, acted as regent. A military coup overthrew Paul in 1941 and proclaimed 17-year-old Peter to be of age to rule. When the Axis Powers forces invaded Yugoslavia less than a month later, Peter fled with his government-in-exile to London. He finished his education at Cambridge University and was commissioned in the Royal Air Force. In 1942, he made a diplomatic visit to the United States in hopes of securing support for Yugoslavia. The petition was unsuccessful.

Peter II married Princess Alexandra of Greece and Denmark in 1944, and she became the last queen of Yugoslavia. Unfortunately, she had a crown but no kingdom. Peter and Alexandra had one son, Alexander, Crown Prince of Yugoslavia, born in

**King Peter II of Yugoslavia (third from right) with Tesla (center) in January 1944.** *Tesla Universe*

1945. As they lived in exile in London, the young couple kept hoping they would be able to go back to Yugoslavia.

When the country became a Communist dictatorship under Tito, however, they knew they would never be able to return to their homeland as king and queen. They moved to the United States, where they lived until their deaths.

Peter II died in 1970 and was interred at the Saint Sava Monastery Church in Libertyville, Illinois, making him the only European monarch ever to be buried in the United States. Alexandra died in 1993. In 2013, their son, Crown Prince Alexander, had his parents' remains taken to Serbia and reinterred at the family mausoleum.

*I visited Dr. Nicola [sic] Tesla, the world-famous Yugoslav-American scientist, in his apartment in the Hotel New Yorker. After I had greeted him the aged scientist said: "It is my greatest honor. I am glad you are in your youth, and I am content that you will be a great ruler. I believe I will live until you come back to a free Yugoslavia. From your father you have received his last words: 'Guard Yugoslavia.' I am proud to be a Serbian and a Yugoslav. Our people cannot perish. Preserve the unity of all the Yugoslavs—the Serbs, the Croats, and the Slovenes."*

Unfortunately, Tesla would not live to see a free Yugoslavia—or the end of the war he'd hoped to avoid with his technological invention.

## Last Days

In early January 1943, Tesla began to complain of chest pains. As usual, he would not seek medical attention. On January 5, he instructed the cleaning maid to put the Do Not Disturb sign on his door, where it remained for the next two days. He lived on the third floor in Room Number 3327. Early on the morning of January 8, another maid, Alice Monaghan, ignored the sign and entered the room to find the old man dead in his bed, his sunken, emaciated face peaceful.

The police and medical examiner were notified immediately, and the medical examiner placed the time of death at 10:30 PM on January 7, 1943. It was his opinion that Tesla had died peacefully in his

# DEATH MASKS

Creating death masks of a deceased person was a tradition in many countries, but especially in Europe and Africa (mostly Egypt). A death mask is an impression taken of a person's face, using wax or plaster, right after death. In the days before photography, creating a death mask was a means of preserving the person's likeness—almost like a portrait. In more modern times, some masks, like Tesla's, were cast into bronze to create a more permanent object. His death mask was also mounted on a special base, designed by sculptor Onorio Ruotolo. It depicts Tesla's Wardenclyffe power transmission tower, his first AC induction motor, and a Tesla coil.

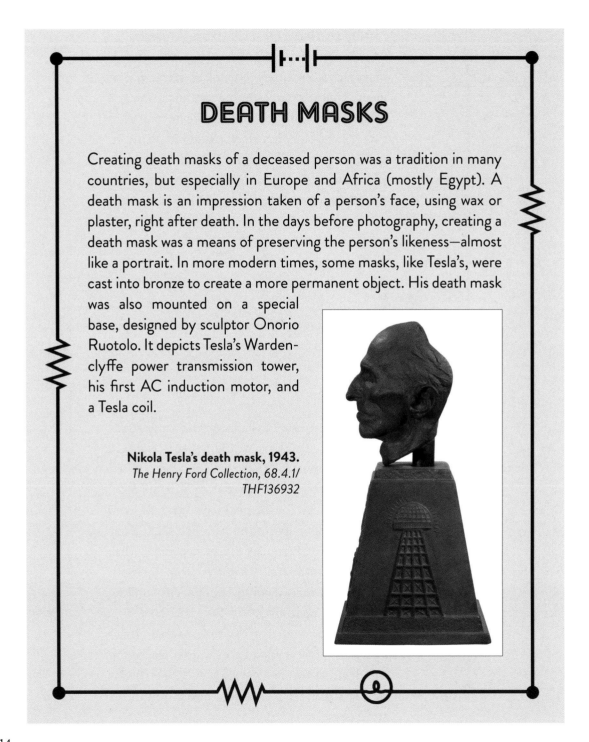

**Nikola Tesla's death mask, 1943.**
*The Henry Ford Collection, 68.4.1/*
*THF136932*

sleep from a heart attack. The examiner also noted that he'd found no suspicious circumstances surrounding the death, and the body was transferred to Campbell's Funeral Parlor at Madison Avenue and 81st Street. Tesla was 86 years old.

A grand state funeral was held for the esteemed inventor on Tuesday, January 12, 1943, at the Cathedral of St. John the Divine. More than 2,000 mourners were present, including other inventors, scientists, dignitaries, friends, and, of course, Tesla's nephew Sava and his loyal writer friend Kenneth Swezey. The service was presided over by prominent Serbian Orthodox priests, and several of the honorary pall bearers were Nobel Prize winners. New York mayor Fiorello La Guardia read a moving eulogy over the radio. President Franklin D. Roosevelt and First Lady Eleanor Roosevelt and other important dignitaries from all over the world sent condolences.

Tesla's publishing friend Hugo Gernsback commissioned Tesla's death mask and wrote of the inventor: "The world, as we run it today, did not appreciate his peculiar greatness."

Fellow inventor and radio pioneer Edwin Howard Armstrong was also in attendance at Tesla's funeral. He commented, "The world, I think, will wait a long time for Nikola Tesla's equal in achievement and imagination."

And US vice president Henry Wallace's personal tribute would have assuredly won Tesla's approval with these words: "Nikola Tesla, Yugoslav born, so lived his life as to make it an outstanding sample of that power which makes the United States not merely an English-speaking nation but a nation with universal appeal. In Nikola Tesla's death the common man loses one of his best friends."

Even though it was not a traditional Serbian Orthodox practice, Sava had his uncle's remains cremated. Tesla's ashes were kept in the United States for 15 years, until after Sava's death in 1956. His personal assistant, Charlotte Muzar, personally delivered them to Belgrade in June 1957. The ashes are now stored in a spherical urn that is on display in the Nikola Tesla Museum in Belgrade.

**The urn that holds Nikola Tesla's ashes.** *Wikimedia Commons*

## A Legacy Shrouded in Mystery

The morning after Tesla's death, Sava Kosanović, accompanied by several other friends and associates, went to Room 3327 at the New Yorker Hotel with the intent of retrieving his uncle's numerous papers and belongings and to see if he'd left a will. Kosanović claimed that when he arrived, he found that many of Tesla's technical papers and a specific black notebook with some pages labeled "Government" were missing. He suspected that the FBI had already searched the room after Tesla's death. Nevertheless, he hired a locksmith to open Tesla's safe, but he said he did not find a will.

According to FBI sources, however, agents went to Tesla's room on January 9 to read through his papers to find out if he had anything that could help in the war effort. One of Tesla's electrical engineering friends even informed them that among the inventor's papers were complete plans for his death ray, along with explanations of how the thing worked.

They found that Kosanović and the others had already entered the room and opened the safe. The agents claimed that Tesla's nephew had taken important papers, and they were worried that dangerous information might fall into the wrong hands, as they suspected Kosanović of having Communist ties. At this point, the Office of Alien Property (OAP) Custodian took over the case from the FBI and seized all of Tesla's papers and property from the New Yorker Hotel. "Two truckloads of paper, furniture, and artifacts were added to some thirty barrels and bundles that had [already] been in storage since the 1930s." Everything was sealed and stored at the Manhattan Storage and Warehouse Company. Because Tesla was an American citizen, this was highly unusual.

Tesla's papers were investigated for three days, and US Navy personnel microfilmed papers they thought might be of interest. Included was Tesla's unpublished article entitled, "The New Art of Projecting Concentrated Non-Dispersive Energy Through Natural Media," which outlined how to create a nondispersive beam of particles. According to biographer Nigel Cawthorne, this was "classified top secret and distributed to Naval Intelligence, the National Defense Research Council, the FBI, MIT, Wright-Patterson Air Force Base and, probably, the White House."

In the end, however, Dr. John G. Trump, a member of the National Defense Research Committee of the Office of Scientific Research and Development who'd also been called in to assist the OAP, decided that there was nothing among Tesla's papers that would be of value to the US military—or "constitute a hazard in unfriendly hands." Trump admitted that he did not bother to open many of Tesla's trunks, and for many years there were lingering rumors of a missing death ray model. Regardless, Trump advised the OAP that he saw no reason to hold on to the inventor's belongings.

By 1950, Tesla's papers and possessions still had not been officially released to Sava Kosanović due to alleged non-payment of back taxes, and he began making official requests to retrieve them. He wanted to send all his uncle's things to the Tesla Museum in Belgrade, but it was not until two years later that he was able to ship the entire 80 trunks of Tesla's papers, equipment, and personal possessions to Yugoslavia. This estate included more than 50 years of research work and records of 5,000 experiments.

## Project Nick and Speculation

Even after World War II, however, there was still interest in Tesla's ideas for a particle beam weapon. In fact, when his papers were sent to Wright-Patterson Air Force Base in Dayton, Ohio, it sparked Project Nick. In 1945, this operation was set in motion to test the feasibility of Tesla's concept for the particle beam weapon, and it was commanded by Brigadier General Laurence C. Craigie.

Apparently, the operation was disbanded within a year, but there was no paper trail of any kind—no published test results or memorandum about the outcome of Project Nick. In fact, all the copies of Tesla's scientific papers seemed to vanish into thin air after this project. Even though the originals had been sent to Belgrade, there were still those who were curious about Tesla's materials and his supposed death ray. But when the FBI received numerous requests from scientists and researchers for Tesla's papers, the agency denied it had them.

Many people wanted to know what had happened to the microfilm copies made during the initial investigation. Conspiracy? Cover up? No, but that did not stop the speculation and rumors.

We now know that the FBI did keep copies of Tesla's papers in a classified library at a US defense research agency, and that the FBI and other government officials were genuinely interested in his particle beam weapons research. The partially redacted (blacked out) declassified documents were finally released under the Freedom of Information Act in 2016, 73 years after the inventor died.

# The Man Behind the Curtain

At the end of World War II, the Soviet Union wanted to block itself from all Western contact, interference, and influence. That's how the "Iron Curtain" came to be. It was the boundary dividing Europe into two different areas based on military factions, political parties, beliefs, and ideals, and it effectively cut off all interaction and exchange of information between people on either side of the barrier. Censorship and propaganda on the Soviet side of the dividing line was common, and Westerners (primarily people in Western Europe or North America) were not usually allowed to enter or have access to resources, papers, or information in the Eastern European countries that were behind the Iron Curtain.

Unfortunately, the country of Yugoslavia and the city of Belgrade were also subjected to a high degree of Communist control all through the Cold War years. This meant that access to Tesla's papers and ideas was essentially denied to all American reporters or scientists until the late 1980s and early 1990s when the Iron Curtain fell and the Soviet Union collapsed. In fact, Yugoslavia's Communist leader Josip Tito specifically forbade Western journalists from visiting the Tesla Museum.

It's not surprising that Tesla's name and legacy faded from memory as each generation of Americans who had known about him and his work passed away. While almost everyone continued to recognize and praise the names of Westinghouse, Marconi, Edison, and Einstein, Nikola Tesla's name was forgotten and left out of history books. And although Tesla's nephews did try to ensure their uncle's work would be remembered, and they helped establish a museum in his honor, the fact remains that the inventor never married or had children. Having direct descendants could've also made a difference in keeping his legacy alive, as was the case with many other famous scientists and inventors.

In the last 20 years, however, interest in the inventor has revived, and Tesla is slowly receiving the attention and accolades that he was denied for so long after his death. The information in history books is being corrected, and people everywhere are learning about Tesla's amazing contributions in the fields of science and technology.

# Supreme Court Decision Reversals

One of Tesla's greatest battles was settled after his death, and it would have been a victory he would have celebrated. On June 21, 1943, the US Supreme Court reversed its 1904 decision awarding Guglielmo Marconi the patent for the invention of the radio. The decision was said to have been made based on Tesla's 1893 lectures on radio transmission and the fact that Marconi would have had to pirate several of Tesla's patents to invent his version of the wireless radio. Patent number 645,576 was awarded back to Tesla. The claims of other inventors, such as Sir Oliver Lodge and John Stone, who felt Marconi had infringed upon their patents as well, were also examined during the case.

Marconi's company, the Marconi Wireless Telegraph Company of America, started the whole

# HOW DOES A MAGLEV TRAIN WORK?

*Nikola Tesla worked a great deal with magnetism, and the magnetic properties he explored are today used for maglev (magnetic levitation) trains. Magnets have two poles—north and south. Opposite poles attract, and like poles repel each other. Maglev trains utilize the like poles to "float" along guideways, rather than resting on tracks, ensuring passengers enjoy a smooth ride.*

*Magnets are also used along the guideway to propel the train forward. They can be made to alternate between north and south to both pull the train (with opposite poles) and push the train (with like poles).*

*Find out for yourself how the maglev train hovers over its guideway.*

------------------------------------------------------------

## You'll Need

⚡ Thin piece of wood such as a wooden ruler

⚡ 2 bar magnets

⚡ Duct tape

1. Place a thin piece of wood between the two magnets, with like poles on top of each other. The magnets will want to repel each other and move apart.

2. Holding the magnets and wood tightly together, wrap them with just enough duct tape to keep the assembly together.

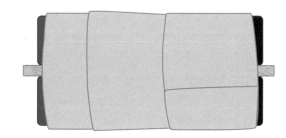

3. Gently tug to remove the piece of wood from between the magnets. The tape should keep the magnets in place.

4. Put the magnets on a flat surface and press down on the top magnet. What do you feel? You've just discovered the powers of magnetic levitation!

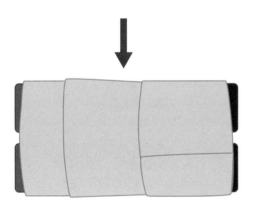

**A maglev train.** *Wikimedia Commons*

thing when it sued the US government early in 1943 for infringement of patents used during World War I. The government countersued, and the hearing went to the Supreme Court. Some historians say that the court declared Marconi's radio patent invalid to keep the US government from having to pay royalties on Marconi's patents. Whatever the reason, Tesla would have been pleased. But unfortunately, since the US Supreme Court's decision happened during World War II, the news got buried in the back pages of newspapers and many people never read or heard about the patent reversal. To this day, most history books still erroneously call Marconi the "Father of Radio."

## Tesla Takes

Although Nikola Tesla has not always been adequately credited for his scientific and innovative contributions, there have been some unique ways he's been remembered. In 1956, a centennial congress was held in Belgrade to celebrate Tesla's life and accomplishments. The 1922 Nobel Prize winner and "Father of Quantum Physics," Niels Bohr, gave a speech and praised Tesla's invention of the polyphase transmission of electric power and research of high-frequency oscillations.

In the same year, the Yugoslav government issued a commemorative Tesla stamp and placed him on the 100-dinar note, and statues and busts were dedicated at museums in his honor.

At the 1960 General Conference on Weights and Measures in France, a new unit, called the tesla (symbol T) was announced. The tesla measures magnetic flux, or magnetic field strength in the International System of Units (SI).

In addition, there has been an asteroid, a moon crater, schools, streets, museums, cars, and an airport named for him. There are awards, conferences, magazines, exhibits, organizations, memorials, plaques, clubs, foundations, computer games, fan clubs, and websites created in his honor, and movies, documentaries, books, and articles about him. There are also Tesla coils on display in many science museums. Moreover, the United States

**The statue of Nikola Tesla on Goat Island, Niagara Falls.**
*Wikimedia Commons*

**The monument of Nikola Tesla at Queen Victoria Park on the Canadian side of the falls.** *Wikimedia Commons*

also issued a commemorative stamp of Tesla and other scientists in the 1980s.

Perhaps one of the most touching Tesla tributes is at Niagara Falls, where Tesla's alternating current system helped establish the first hydroelectric plant. There are two statues to remember the inventor's contributions. The first is on Goat Island on the American side of the falls. It was a gift from the Yugoslav government to the United States in 1976, created by the Croatian sculptor Frano Kršinić. It is a copy of the statue that is at the electrical engineering building at the University of Belgrade in Serbia, which shows Tesla in sitting position, reading blueprints.

The other Tesla statue is on the Canadian side of the falls and was unveiled in 2006 to commemorate Tesla's 150th birthday. This impressive monument depicts Tesla in tux and tails, holding a top hat and standing atop one of his alternating current motors. The statue also captures the moment when Tesla supposedly scratched the design for his AC motor into the dirt. It was created by Canadian sculptor Les Drysdale and is positioned so that Tesla gazes out over Horseshoe Falls.

# EXPLORE STEM CAREERS

*Nikola Tesla was a prolific inventor, physicist, scientist, mathematician, and electrical engineer. He was intelligent, but he also spent hours studying, learning, and perfecting his skills. He was a very hard worker. Today, Tesla's field of work would be referred to as a STEM career—Science, Technology, Engineering, and Math.*

*Why not explore STEM careers for yourself? There are many fascinating jobs within these areas, and you might just be inspired to pursue a certain STEM career in the future! Jot down the ones that interest you.*

---

## You'll Need

⚡ Library or internet access

⚡ Paper and pencil, or computer

Here are some examples of interesting STEM careers you can investigate, but there are many, many more:

Artificial intelligence

Astronomy

Biology

Cartography

Chemistry

Engineering (Electrical, Aerospace, Mechanical, Biochemical, Nuclear, Environmental, etc.)

Mathematics

Medical science

Meteorology

Physics

Robotics

Software development

Solar energy

Statistics

Wind energy

Additionally, here are a few websites that give more information about STEM careers:

**Science Buddies:** www.sciencebuddies.org/science-engineering-careers

**Kids Ahead:** http://kidsahead.com

**National Geographic—NASA for Kids:** www.nationalgeographic.org/media/nasa-kids-intro-engineering

**National Academy of Engineering—Engineer Girl:** www.engineergirl.org

**NASA:** www.nasa.gov

1. Select a STEM career that most interests you.

2. With the consent and assistance of a teacher or parent, contact and interview an individual who works in a STEM job. Here are a few basic interview questions to get you started:

   ❯ What part of your job do you like best? Least?

   ❯ What school subjects did you study to prepare you for your job?

   ❯ What do you wish you'd known before you pursued this career?

   ❯ What advice can you give to someone interested in pursuing the same career?

3. Come up with four or five more questions of your own to ask.

Do you think you'd like to have a STEM career?

## Recap and Remembrance

Nikola Tesla lived an extraordinary life. From his humble beginnings in a faraway land to his last days in a fashionable New York hotel, he never stopped creating, inventing, and envisioning what could be. He truly longed to make a difference in the world and help humankind. His experiments and inventions laid the groundwork for future technology, and he made many predictions about the future that have since come to pass.

Of course, some of his plans and inventions never panned out and not all his theories were correct. Even so, scientists still like to discuss his ideas (especially the ones that seem impossible or far off the mark) even today. And who knows? Some of his crazy-sounding ideas and concepts may still come to pass in the future. After all, many of his ideas and inventions have already been incorporated into our modern high-tech world. Yes, he was a man too far ahead of *his* time, but he certainly has influenced the way we live in *our* time.

Delusional dreamer, mad scientist, quirky old man? Sometimes. Bold thinker, brilliant inventor, history changer, visionary? Always.

> *Let the future tell the truth and evaluate each one according to his work and accomplishments. The present is theirs, the future, for which I really worked, is mine.*
> **—Nikola Tesla**

# ACKNOWLEDGMENTS

I would like to thank my editors, past and present, Lisa Reardon, Jerome Pohlen, and Ellen Hornor, and all the other great people at Chicago Review Press for helping me bring the quirky, eccentric, imaginative, prescient, and undeniably intelligent Nikola Tesla to life. It was not an easy task to distill his amazing story and accomplishments into seven chapters. Thanks also to my favorite librarians, Deborah Moorman and Victoria Horst, for their unwavering assistance and encouragement—and for helping me track down the most obscure sources. A big shout-out to Cameron Prince of Tesla Universe for his patience and help in acquiring many of the images I needed for the book. Cameron has created an excellent resource of all things Tesla, and the information and resources on Tesla Universe were invaluable to me during my research phase.

In remembrance of Janice Carlisle, Irwin Academy teacher, who fostered my love of science and put up with all my talking and endless questions.

To my parents, Edward and Betty McIntyre; my sister and traveling buddy, Mindy McHugh; my "in-loves," Roger and Peggy O'Quinn; and all the rest of my friends and family for their continued support and interest in my writing projects. And, of course, thank you to my husband, Chad, and our children, Erin, Elisabeth, Wesley, Ellie, John, and Alexander, for cheering me on—and prodding me into action when necessary. I love you!

# RESOURCES TO EXPLORE

## BOOKS

Cole, Joanna, and Bruce Degen. *The Magic School Bus and the Electric Field Trip.* New York: Scholastic, 1997.

Rusch, Elizabeth. *Electrical Wizard: How Nikola Tesla Lit Up the World.* Somerville, MA: Candlewick, 2013.

## FILMS AND VIDEOS

"Tesla," on *American Experience* (PBS, 2016), www.pbs.org/wgbh/americanexperience/films/tesla.

*Tesla: Master of Lightning* (PBS, 2000), www.pbs.org/tesla/index.html.

## PLACES TO VISIT, IN PERSON OR ONLINE

Nikola Tesla Memorial Center and Birthplace: www.mcnikolatesla.hr
Nikola Tesla Museum: www.nikolateslamuseum.org
SPARK Museum of Electrical Invention: www.sparkmuseum.org
Tesla at Niagara Museum: www.teslaniagara.org
Tesla Memorial Society of New York: www.teslasociety.com
Tesla Science Center at Wardenclyffe: www.teslasciencecenter.org
Tesla Science Foundation: www.teslasciencefoundation.org
Tesla Universe: https://teslauniverse.com

# NOTES

## Introduction

*"Land of Golden Promise"*: Nikola Tesla, *My Inventions and Other Writings* (New York: Dover, 2016), 33.

## Chapter 1: Electrified Beginnings

*"He'll be a child of the storm"*: Nigel Cawthorne, *Tesla: The Life and Times of an Electric Messiah* (New York: Chartwell Books, 2014), 11.

*"No, a child of light"*: Cawthorne, *Life and Times*, 11.

*"social equality among peoples"*: Marc J. Seifer, *Wizard: The Life and Times of Nikola Tesla, Biography of a Genius* (New York: Citadel Press Books, 1998), 6.

*"My mother descended"*: Nikola Tesla, *My Inventions and Other Writings* (New York: Dover, 2016), 4.

*"My mother was an inventor"*: Tesla, *My Inventions*, 4.

*"the fountain of my enjoyment"*: Margaret Cheney and Robert Uth, *Tesla: Master of Lightning* (New York: Barnes and Noble Publishing, 1999), 4.

*"Mačak's back was a sheet"*: Cheney and Uth, *Tesla*, 4.

*"two teeth protruding"*: Tesla, *My Inventions*, 2.

*"This here is not as ugly"*: Tesla, *My Inventions*, 3.

*"I never had seen a hook"*: M. K. Wisehart, "Making Your Imagination Work for You," *American Magazine*, April 1921, 13.

*"That disgusting sight terminated"*: Tesla, *My Inventions*, 16.

*"The recollection of [Dane's]"*: Tesla, *My Inventions*, 2.

*"calamity"*: Tesla, *My Inventions*, 17.

*"In our new house"*: Tesla, *My Inventions*, 17.

*"In my boyhood I suffered"*: Tesla, *My Inventions*, 4.

*"the result of a reflex"*: Tesla, *My Inventions*, 4.

*"funeral or some such"*: Tesla, *My Inventions*, 5.

*"flit away"*: Tesla, *My Inventions*, 5.

*"Every night (and sometimes"*: Tesla, *My Inventions*, 5.

*"violent aversion"*: Tesla, *My Inventions*, 8.

*"I counted the steps"*: Tesla, *My Inventions*, 8.

*"onion-shaped dome"*: W. Bernard Carlson, *Tesla: Inventor of the Electrical Age.* (Princeton, NJ: Princeton University Press, 2013), 21.

*"He was practically ostracized"*: John J. O'Neill, *Prodigal Genius: The Life of Nikola Tesla* (Albuquerque, NM: Brotherhood of Life, 1994), 25.

*"Tesla learned that solving"*: Carlson, *Tesla*, 26.

*"I began to discipline myself"*: Michael Burgan, *Nikola Tesla: Physicist, Inventor, Electrical Engineer* (Minneapolis, MN: Compass Point Books, 2009), 24.

*"doing as [he] willed"*: Tesla, *My Inventions*, 9.

*"In his imagination"*: Margaret Cheney, *Tesla: Man Out of Time* (New York: Touchstone, 1981), 36.

*"I was interested in electricity"*: Seifer, *Wizard*, 13.

*"[I] was prostrated"*: Tesla, *My Inventions*, 21.

*"a few volumes of new literature"*: Tesla, *My Inventions*, 21.

*"the miraculous recovery"*: Tesla, *My Inventions*, 21.

*"burst into tears"*: Tesla, *My Inventions*, 21.

*"an old war horse"*: Tesla, *My Inventions*, 22.

*"very delicate"*: Tesla, *My Inventions*, 22.

*"atmosphere of refinement"*: Tesla, *My Inventions*, 22.

*"streets were stacked with corpses"*: Seifer, *Wizard*, 14.

*"Perhaps I may get well"*: Burgan, *Nikola Tesla*, 25.

*"bitter decoction"*: Tesla, *My Inventions*, 23.

*"I came to life like"*: Tesla, *My Inventions*, 23.

*"stronger in body"*: Tesla, *My Inventions*, 23.

"submarine tube": Lisa J. Aldrich, *Nikola Tesla and the Taming of Electricity* (Greensboro, NC: Morgan Reynolds, 2005), 25.

"Military Frontier Administration Authority (Grenzlandsverwaltungsbehoerde)": Carlson, *Tesla*, 32.

"give his parents a surprise": Tesla, *My Inventions*, 24.

"I regularly started my work": Tesla, *My Inventions*, 24.

"made light of these": Tesla, *My Inventions*, 24.

"Mr. Tesla may accomplish": Tesla, *My Inventions*, 25.

"undertook the task": Tesla, *My Inventions*, 26.

"vagrant": Carlson, *Tesla*, 47.

"One afternoon, I remember": Tesla, *My Inventions*, 9.

## Chapter 2: Moving to America

"complete breakdown of nerves": Tesla, *My Inventions*, 26.

"could hear the ticking": Cheney, *Man Out of Time*, 42.

"the air itself hurt": D. Mrkich, *Nikola Tesla: The European Years (1856–1884)* (Ottawa, ON: Commoners, 2010), 102.

"The glow retreats, done": Johann Wolfgang von Goethe, *Faust*, Part I, translated by Bayard Taylor (New York: Columbia University Press, 1908), 39.

"As I uttered these inspiring words": Tesla, *My Inventions*, 28.

"The images were wonderfully sharp": Tesla, *My Inventions*, 28.

"It was a mental state": Tesla, *My Inventions*, 28.

"threw himself into improving": Carlson, *Tesla*, 63.

"the last twenty-nine days": Inez Hunt and W. W. Draper, *Lightning in His Hand: The Life Story of Nikola Tesla* (Hawthorne, CA: Omni, 1964), 35.

"pleasing anticipations" . . . "liberal compensation": Tesla, *My Inventions*, 32.

"finally had the satisfaction": Tesla, *My Inventions*, 31.

"a castle in Spain": Tesla, *My Inventions*, 33.

"Land of Golden Promise": Tesla, *My Inventions*, 33.

"I know two great men": O'Neill, *Prodigal Genius*, 67.

"The meeting with Edison": Tesla, *My Inventions*, 34.

"Thomas Alva Edison was": Seifer, *Wizard*, 35.

"our Parisian": Tesla, *My Inventions*, 34.

"had full freedom": Tesla, *My Inventions*, 34.

"There's fifty thousand dollars": O'Neill, *Prodigal Genius*, 70.

"Tesla, you don't understand": O'Neill, *Prodigal Genius*, 70.

"Tesla arc lamp which": Cheney, *Man Out of Time*, 59.

"no flickering and hissing": Seifer, *Wizard*, 41.

"handsomely engraved stock certificate": Cheney, *Man Out of Time*, 59.

"lived through a year": O'Neill, *Prodigal Genius*, 71.

"seemed a mockery" . . . "resented the utter waste": O'Neill, *Prodigal Genius*, 71.

"influence the course": Seifer, *Wizard*, 43.

"A rotating field magnet": Hugo Gernsback, "Tesla's Egg of Columbus," *Electrical Experimenter*, March 1919, 775.

"one of the most influential": Seifer, *Wizard*, 44.

"mysterious" . . . "choreograph Tesla's entrée": Seifer, *Wizard*, 44.

"Tesla's lecture, and": O'Neill, *Prodigal Genius*, 75.

## Chapter 3: Roadblocks and Victories

"There is no doubt that Edison": Hunt and Draper, *Lightning in His Hand*, 48.

"As Edison saw it": Cheney, *Man Out of Time*, 65.

"the stench of burning": Mark Essig, *Edison and the Electric Chair: A Story of Light and Death* (New York: Walker, 2003), 253.

"ten hangings than": Seifer, *Wizard*, 58.

"literally roasted alive": Jill Jonnes, *Empires of Light: Edison, Tesla, Westinghouse, and the Race to Electrify the World* (New York: Random House, 2003), 213.

"something of a society darling": Jonnes, *Empires of Light*, 312.

"never hesitated to face": O'Neill, *Prodigal Genius*, 85.

"George Westinghouse was": O'Neill, *Prodigal Genius*, 89.

"weird, storklike figure": Cheney, *Man Out of Time*, 76.

"We are whirling through": Jonnes, *Empires of Light*, 232.

"stopper lamps": Seifer, *Wizard*, 100.

"All told, twenty-seven million": Jonnes, *Empires of Light*, 265.

## Chapter 4: From Waterfalls to Wardenclyffe

"with a victory": Cheney, *Man Out of Time*, 119.

"transmitted radio waves": Cheney and Uth, *Tesla*, 42.

"small portable radio": Jonnes, *Empires of Light*, 314.

"manufacture and sell machinery": Jonnes, *Empires of Light*, 316.

"from a gas jet" . . . "means of producing": Cheney, *Man Out of Time*, 129.

"their contributions to the development": "The Nobel Prize in Physics 1909," Nobel Prize website, www.nobelprize.org/prizes/physics/1909/summary.

"mission of friendly courtesy": Tom Miller, "Remember the Maine," *Smithsonian Magazine*, February 1, 1998, www.smithsonianmag.com/history/remember-the-maine-56071873.

"small, odd-looking": Cheney and Uth, *Tesla*, 79.

"could attack and destroy": Cheney, *Man Out of Time*, 162.

"wild fancy": Alden P. Armagnac, "A Famous Prophet of Science Looks into the Future," *Popular Science Monthly*, November 1928, 17.

"producing 4,000,000 volts": Cheney and Uth, *Tesla*, 170.

"devised a telescoping": Carlson, *Tesla*, 267.

"to be free of the disturbing": Seifer, *Wizard*, 215.

"power a device capable": Cheney, *Man Out of Time*, 173.

"magnifying transmitter": Tesla, *My Inventions*, 41.

"resonant transformer": Tesla, *My Inventions*, 41.

"anticipate the ridicule": Cheney, *Man Out of Time*, 190.

"Martian theory": Aldrich, *Taming of Electricity*, 114.

"from the stars via": Aldrich, *Taming of Electricity*, 115.

"The same principle may": "Is Tesla to Signal the Stars?" *Electrical World*, April 4, 1896, 369.

"Residents watched in awe": Cheney, *Man Out of Time*, 207.

## Chapter 5: Trials, Successes, and Sadness

"Troubles and troubles": Cheney, *Man Out of Time*, 215.

"My flying machine": Nikola Tesla, as told to Frank Parker Stockbridge, "Tesla's New Monarch of Mechanics," *New York Herald*, October 15, 1911.

"their contributions to the development of wireless telegraphy": "The Nobel Prize in Physics 1909," Nobel Prize website, www.nobelprize.org /prizes/physics/1909/summary.

## Chapter 6: Through the Years: 1914–1931

"His was a wonderful": Nikola Tesla, tribute to George Westinghouse, *Electrical World*, March 21, 1914, 637.

"a weapon of sufficient magnitude": Cheney and Uth, *Tesla*, 125.

"the world had officially": Seifer, *Wizard*, 382.

"he began the slow": Seifer, *Wizard*, 382.

"wearing a crown": O'Neill, *Prodigal Genius*, 236.

"We asked Mr. Tesla": O'Neill, *Prodigal Genius*, 237.

"fluid flow tube": Seifer, *Wizard*, 398.

"oozed charm and wit": Seifer, *Wizard*, 399.

"an unusual tale": Seifer, *Wizard*, 399.

"As I looked at her": O'Neill, *Prodigal Genius*, 317.

"acknowledged with respect": Cheney, *Man Out of Time*, 293.

"When I say a new source": "Tesla at 75," *Time*, July 20, 1931, 27.

"in a few months": "Tesla at 75," 27.

"It is improbable that": "Tesla at 75," 27.

## Chapter 7: Quiet Departures

"problem of obtaining power": Nikola Tesla, "Our Future Motive Power," *Everyday Science and Mechanics*, December 1931, 230–36.

"technical problems could be solved": Cheney, *Man Out of Time*, 297.

"As is typical of": Cheney, *Man Out of Time*, 298.

"end droughts, forest fires": Burgan, *Nikola Tesla*, 90.

"their former champion out": Seifer, *Wizard*, 435.

"generous tips to those": Cawthorne, *Life and Times*, 166.

"which may be relatively": Nikola Tesla, quoted in George Sylvester Viereck, "A Machine to End War," *Liberty*, February 1935.

"was talking sense or nonsense": Cheney, *Man Out of Time*, 305.

"if no country [could]": Tesla, quoted in Viereck, "Machine to End War," 7.

"the apparatus could send": "Tesla, at 78, Bares New 'Death Beam,'" *New York Times*, July 11, 1934.

"would surround each country" . . . "could be generated": "Tesla, at 78," *New York Times*.

"supply plans, specifications" . . . "Soviet scientists and engineers": Carlson, *Tesla*, 388.

"It seems that I have": Tesla, quoted in Viereck, "Machine to End War," *Liberty Magazine*, February 1935, 5.

"much like an eagle" . . . "read a prepared": Seifer, *Wizard*, 441.

"Of course you couldn't": O'Neill, *Prodigal Genius*, 274.

"The inventor may have been brilliant": Matt Novak, "Nikola Tesla the Eugenicist: Eliminating Undesirables by 2100," Smithsonian.com, November 16, 2012, www.smithsonianmag.com/history /nikola-tesla-the-eugenicist-eliminating-unde sirables-by-2100-130299355/#zkHsoWugRSqkp t5W.99.

"revolutionary struggle": Cheney and Uth, *Tesla*, 153.

"I visited Dr. Nicola": Peter II of Yugoslavia quoted in Cheney, *Tesla*, 321.

"The world, as we run": Seifer, *Wizard*, 444.

"The world, I think": Aleksandar S. Marincic, "The Tesla Museum," Tesla Memorial Society of New York, http://teslasociety.com/tmuseum.htm.

"Nikola Tesla, Yugoslav born": "2,000 Are Present at Tesla Funeral," *New York Times*, January 13, 1943.

"Two truckloads": Cheney and Uth, *Tesla*, 158.

"classified top secret": Cawthorne, *Life and Times*, 177.

"constitute a hazard": Cheney, *Man Out of Time*, 335.

# SELECTED BIBLIOGRAPHY

Titles marked with an asterisk are especially appropriate for young readers.

*Aldrich, Lisa J. *Nikola Tesla and the Taming of Electricity*. Greensboro, NC: Morgan Reynolds, 2005.

*Burgan, Michael. *Nikola Tesla: Physicist, Inventor, Electrical Engineer*. Signature Lives Series. Minneapolis, MN: Compass Point Books, 2009.

Carlson, W. Bernard. *Tesla: Inventor of the Electrical Age*. Princeton, NJ: Princeton University Press, 2013.

*Cawthorne, Nigel. *Tesla vs Edison: The Life-Long Feud That Electrified the World*. New York: Chartwell Books, 2016.

*Cawthorne, Nigel. *Tesla: The Life and Times of an Electric Messiah*. New York: Chartwell Books, 2014.

Cheney, Margaret. *Tesla: Man Out of Time*. New York: Touchstone, 1981.

Cheney, Margaret, and Robert Uth. *Tesla: Master of Lightning*. New York: Barnes and Noble Publishing, 1999.

Essig, Mark. *Edison and the Electric Chair: A Story of Light and Death*. New York: Walker, 2003.

Hunt, Inez, and W. W. Draper. *Lightning in His Hand: The Life Story of Nikola Tesla*. Hawthorne, CA: Omni, 1964 (reprinted 1981).

Jonnes, Jill. *Empires of Light: Edison, Tesla, Westinghouse, and the Race to Electrify the World*. New York: Random House, 2003.

*Kent, David J. *Tesla: The Wizard of Electricity*. New York: Fall River, 2013.

Mrkich, D. *Nikola Tesla: The European Years (1856–1884)*. Men's Culture and History Series. Ottawa, ON: Commoners, 2010.

O'Neill, John J. *Prodigal Genius: The Life of Nikola Tesla*. Albuquerque, NM: Brotherhood of Life, 1994 (reprinted 1996).

Seifer, Marc J. *Wizard: The Life and Times of Nikola Tesla, Biography of a Genius*. New York: Citadel Press Books, 1998 (reprinted 2016).

Tesla, Nikola. *My Inventions and Other Writings*. New York: Dover, 2016.

Wasik, John F. *Lightning Strikes: Timeless Lessons in Creativity from the Life and Work of Nikola Tesla*. New York: Sterling, 2016.

# INDEX